The Adventures of Charlie Pierce

The Last Calusa

by Harvey E. Oyer III

Illustrations by James Balkovek, MFA

Map Illustration by Jeanne Brady

www.TheAdventuresofCharliePierce.com
Become a friend of Charlie Pierce on **Facebook**
Facebook.com/CharliePierceBooks

 MIDDLE
RIVER
PRESS

ISBN 978-0-9857295-2-3

Published by:
Middle River Press
Oakland Park, Florida
middleriverpress.com
info@middleriverpress.com
Printed in the U.S.A.
Fifth printing

Atlantic Ocean

Palm Beach
Hypoluxo Island
Boca Raton Inlet
Miami River
Brickell's Trading Post
Biscayne Bay
Card Sound
Puerto Rico

Lake Okeechobee

Caloosahatchee River
Fort Myers
Everglades
Pa-Hay-Okee
Shark River
Ponce de Leon Bay
Cape Sable
Florida Bay
Florida Keys

Pine Island
Sanibel Island
Ten Thousand Islands

Gulf of Mexico

Cuba

E
N
S
W

Florida
Miami

La Busqueda de Ponce de Leon y la Fuente de Juventud

Dedication

To my wonderful sisters, Susan and Christian, for their lifetime of love and support.

Acknowledgments

I wish to acknowledge the dedicated, outstanding work of editor Jon VanZile, illustrator James Balkovek, MFA, map illustrator Jeanne Brady, and the folks at Middle River Press. I also want to acknowledge the writings of Charles W. Pierce and Lillie Pierce Voss, from which I take many of the stories contained herein. My special thanks to David Lawrence, Jr., Pat Kissel, and Dr. William H. Marquardt for their review of the manuscript and helpful suggestions.

Introduction

This is the third book in a series of books about the adventures of young Charlie Pierce, one of South Florida's earliest pioneer settlers. The story follows teenage Charlie and his fearless little sister Lillie in the late 1800s, when South Florida was America's last frontier. Together with his Seminole friend, Tiger, Charlie experienced one of the most intriguing and exotic lives imaginable. His adventures as a young boy growing up in the wild, untamed jungles of Florida became legendary. Perhaps no other person experienced firsthand as many important events and met as many influential characters in South Florida's history.

For more information about the Pierce family's adventures, go to

www.TheAdventuresofCharliePierce.com
Become a friend of Charlie Pierce on **Facebook**
Facebook.com/CharliePierceBooks

Table of Contents

Chapter One

Pineapples for Violins

"Pineapples, Charlie. The future is pineapples."

This is what Uncle Will said when we made our deal. But now I wondered if he'd ever planted a pineapple in his life. Probably not.

Still, Uncle Will seemed mighty sure of himself. He said farmers were rushing to plant acres of pineapples from Melbourne to the Keys, and he wanted to get in on the ground floor.

"Ground floor," I muttered to myself. "More like ground dirt."

I had good cause to be in a foul mood. Summer was coming soon, and the sun stood high up in the sky and beat down on me like a flame. Worse yet, I'd agreed to plant six thousand pineapple slips, and I wasn't even half done yet. My hands were bleeding, and I had deep scratches up my arms.

I'd seen a lot of unfriendly plants in Florida, ones that could sting and leave a rash that would itch for days, but I'd never seen anything as unfriendly as the pineapple. The plant had spikes where leaves should have been, no roots to speak of, and they were devilishly tricky to plant. To start, I had to stretch a line down each row where the plants would be set. Then I'd drop a little pineapple slip every eighteen inches along the line. Finally, I'd go back with a special stick called a dibber and push them down into the sand to plant each one.

Problem was, I had no idea how deep to plant them. To be on the safe side, I pushed them down extra deep.

I wouldn't have been planting pineapples at all except that I had my eye on a new violin, and I didn't care that my friend Guy Bradley had already started calling me a fiddlin' fool. Truth was, the violin made the most beautiful music I'd ever heard. So when Uncle Will offered to pay me $1 for every one thousand slips, I jumped at the chance.

Of course, that was before I realized what it was like to plant pineapples.

A shadow fell over my basket of pineapple slips and a voice said, "You're planting them too deep, Charlie. They're gonna die if you bury 'em like that."

I looked back to see my little sister Lillie standing behind me. She was shading the sun with one hand and had her other hand perched on her hip, looking more and more like Mama. Except that her hair was tied into pigtails, which she said was easier for climbing trees so her hair didn't get stuck in her eyes.

"What do you know about it?" I said. "You never planted a pineapple before either."

She shrugged. "Don't believe me then. I'm just saying they're bromeliads and they don't have much of a root system. They get water from above. It fills that little cup in the center."

"Bromawhats? Oh forget it. Why'd you come out here anyway? Shouldn't you be at your lessons with Mama?"

She glanced back at the house, across the mostly empty field. "Mama sent me. You got visitors."

"Visitors? Who is it?"

She shrugged. "Don't know. Cap Dimick just delivered them and they talked to Papa for a bit, then Mama told me to come get you."

I stood up and wiped my hands on my pants. Visitors?

It's true, there were more and more people moving into the lake country, as we all called the area around Lake Worth. We saw more boat traffic on the lake now, and pineapple farmers were clearing fields all along the west shore. Land prices were rising rapidly all along the lake. But even still, it wasn't like we got wagonloads of visitors on the island, especially strangers. Mostly it was my friends Guy and Louis Bradley, and sometimes Tiger Bowlegs, my best friend.

We were lucky, Papa said, that we saved our beloved Hypoluxo Island while we could still afford to. Just the year before, Lillie and I, along with Tiger and the two Bradley brothers, had gone on a hunting expedition deep into Pa-Hay-Okee to make enough money to save the island from foreclosure because of real estate taxes. Our plan was to hunt plume birds and sell the feathers, which were more valuable than gold up in the big northern cities and even in Europe.

When we came back, I gave the money to Papa just as I'd promised I would, but the trip hadn't turned out like we expected. We'd seen the camps full of dead birds, and it was nothing but sad to see crates and crates of skins and feathers shipped out just so ladies could wear feathers on their heads like peacocks. When we got back, I'd promised I'd never kill another plume bird again.

"You coming?" Lillie said. "Or you just gonna stand there? They're waiting."

"They give their names?" I asked.

Lillie shook her head. "Nope. Just that there's two of 'em and they dress nice and they talk funny, like from up north."

"Huh."

I walked with Lillie back toward the house, wondering who had come to see me and what they could want.

13

Chapter Two

Dr. Livingston, I Presume

I found two men sitting at our kitchen table when I walked in. Mama was in the middle of pouring a cup of tea, which was strange enough. We never drank tea in the middle of a hot day. Even stranger, I saw that Mama had brought down her special china teacups she got from her family in Chicago.

I shot Lillie a look, but she just shrugged.

"So," Mama was saying as she set out a little saucer with lump sugar, "you were saying you're from Yale. How impressive!"

Papa was there too. He looked like he'd just come in from working outside. He was dirty and didn't look very happy about sitting inside during the day while these two gentlemen were served on Mama's best china and given our precious lump sugar.

The older of the two men was busy loading a pipe with sweet-smelling tobacco. He didn't look like anybody I'd ever seen. Even the rich men in Florida usually worked outside and their clothes and skin showed it. This man had a perfectly trimmed brown beard, nice leather shoes that still had shine on them, and he wore a tweed jacket with a fancy handkerchief sticking up from the breast pocket.

"Why, yes," he said in a deep voice. "Yale University. Up in Connecticut, ma'am." I swear I thought Mama was going to faint, and Papa looked even more sour. I didn't know much about Yale, except that it was a college for rich people.

Everybody turned to look at me, and I racked my brain to think if I had done anything I could get in trouble for.

"Charlie," Mama said, "this here is Dr. George Livingston. He's a professor from Yale University. A naturalist."

"Charlie!" Dr. Livingston said in his deep voice. "Glad you could join us! I've heard a lot about you, young man."

"Me?" I said, thoroughly confused.

"Indeed. I want to introduce you to my student assistant, Jonathan Bartley."

The second man stood up and stuck out his hand. I shook it and realized that Mr. Bartley couldn't have been much older than me—except that he was dressed in formal britches and a white button-down shirt and he wore small wire-framed glasses that perched on his thin nose. "Charlie," he said, "nice to meet you."

Dr. Livingston produced a match, flicked it casually on the bottom of his shoe, and puffed the ember of his pipe to life. A cloud of perfumed smoke filled the kitchen, and Papa made a strangled sort of noise. No smoking inside was one of Mama's strictest rules.

I was still too shocked and confused to say anything when Dr. Livingston set his pipe down and said, "So Charlie, I'll bet you're wondering why we've traveled all the way down here from Connecticut to visit your delightful island."

"Um, yes, sir," I stammered.

"Jonathan?"

Mr. Bartley leaned over to a case I hadn't noticed on the floor and produced a folder tied with a ribbon. He untied it and handed Dr. Livingston a thick sheaf of papers.

Dr. Livingston laid the packet on the table, then rested his hand on it and looked at me, puffing on his pipe like he was sizing me up. "I have a proposal for you, Mr. Charlie Pierce," he said.

I waited to see what he had to say next.

"A man of few words, eh?" he said. "I respect that. So here it is. I've asked up and down this coast for the best guide into the great swampland that lies south and west of here. And your name, Charlie, your name was the one I heard."

"Me? Who told you that?"

Dr. Livingston glanced at Mr. Bartley. "I believe it was a Captain Armour at the Jupiter Inlet Lighthouse, was it not?"

Mr. Bartley nodded, and I said, "Captain Armour told you that?"

"Yes he did. Said you led an expedition last year deep into the swamp, further than any white man has ever gone. As soon as I heard that, I knew you were the boy I wanted to talk to, the best swamp guide in the whole region."

"Oh, well, I don't know about that, Mr. Livingston—"

"Doctor Livingston, son," he corrected.

"Right. I don't know about that. I mean, my friend, Tiger Bowlegs, is really the one who took us back there. Come to think of it, lots of Seminole already live there."

Dr. Livingston and Mr. Bartley exchanged a quick glance.

"Yes, yes, of course they do," Dr. Livingston said. "But, ah, I have a valuable proposition to make, and I need someone I can trust. Hear me out."

Now Papa sat up and listened. Even Mama paused from her fluttering around.

Dr. Livingston took a long minute opening his packet of papers with a great flourish, then he carefully slid out a small stack of papers. He pushed it across the table so we could all see it. Mr. Bartley's eyes were glued to the stack as Dr. Livingston carefully peeled back the top layer to reveal a dried and pressed flower. Even I could see it was an unusual flower. It was the purest white with long petals that hung down like pigtails.

"You know what that is?" Dr. Livingston asked.

I shrugged and looked at Lillie. I figured if anybody would know, it would be her. But she shrugged back at me.

"It's a *Dendrophylax lindenii*. A ghost orchid, Charlie."

"Oh," I said, still not sure what to make of this strange and very pretty, but also very dead flower.

"Let me explain. These flowers were discovered in the great swamp not too long ago. They grow in the deepest parts of the swamp, sticking to the sides of trees. The plants have no leaves, so the flowers spring forth from the bare roots and hang above the water, hoping to attract a moth with their magnificent bottom petals. You can see them here in dried form, but trust me, Charlie, the real plant would be breathtaking."

"Uh, sure," I said.

"Charlie, do you know much about orchids?" Dr. Livingston asked.

"Can't say that I do," I answered.

"They're the most wonderful of all plants," Mr. Bartley suddenly said, like he couldn't hold it back any longer. "They're the most specialized of all plants, each growing in a very unique environment. And they have the most incredible flowers! Flowers shaped like tubes, flowers shaped like moths, flowers that smell like chocolate. The most popular orchids are epiphytes. They grow with no dirt at all, just their bare roots hanging in the air—"

Dr. Livingston cleared his throat, and Mr. Bartley fell silent. "Right, right," Dr. Livingston said. "But here's the important part. As novel and interesting as these plants are botanically speaking, the English have an insatiable appetite for new specimens. Right now, English orchid hunters are spread out across the globe, throughout all of the world's deepest jungles and most remote valleys, looking for the most exotic and beautiful flowers. Back in England, the Queen herself has ordered construction of the largest glass house in the world at the Kew Royal Botanic Gardens in London to house the royal plant collection. And private collectors have been known to pay a fortune for a single living plant."

A fortune for a flower? Now my ears perked up.

"So, Charlie, here is my proposition. I want to hire you to take myself and Bartley deep into the great swamp, to the habitat where these flowers naturally live, so we can collect them and further our understanding for science."

"Flowers?" I said. "I don't know nothing about flowers."

Mama was too flustered to even correct my English.

"You don't need to know anything about flowers," Dr. Livingston said, gently stressing the word anything. "You can leave that part to us. You just need to get us there."

"Well," I said, thinking, "unless you got a boat of your own, we'd need to outfit one that could make the trip, and it'll cost to get me as a guide—"

"We're prepared to pay you $5 a day, and as for the boat, you just tell us what you'd need, and we'll take care of it."

I was thunderstruck. Five dollars a day! That was twice as much as I was going to ask for. I did a quick calculation in my head and realized I'd have to plant the whole island with pineapples to earn the same as I could in a single day. And when I considered that a journey would take at least three weeks…my heart leaped into my throat. I could easily make $100 or more. And it wasn't like we'd be hunting birds or killing anything. He was just talking about collecting a few flowers.

I glanced at Papa, who looked just as thunderstruck as I did.

I cleared my throat, not wanting to appear too anxious. "Uh, well, it sounds, er, like a fair proposition." But then a new thought occurred to me. There was no way I could get anyone back into

Pa-Hay-Okee by myself. I hadn't been pulling his leg before. Tiger really was the one who found our way the first time.

So I said, "I'd want my friend, Tiger Bowlegs, to come along if he could, 'cause he's, ah, well, his people know the swamps and—"

"Me too," Lillie suddenly put in. Every adult head in the room turned to her. She had her chin set and her arms folded across her chest. "I want to come too."

"Oh Lillie—" Mama started.

"I want to go too!" she insisted again. "I'm better'n Charlie in the woods anyways. You know it's true."

"Now wait just a—" I said.

Dr. Livingston looked amused, but Papa was starting to look worried.

This could shape up to be another knock-down argument between Lillie and Mama, and Papa was always getting stuck between them.

"Lillie," he said quickly, "we'll talk about that later."

"Talk about it later?" she said. "That means you'll say no later."

"Lillie, let us work this out first," Papa said gently. "Then we'll talk about who goes along and who doesn't."

She looked mollified, at least for the time being, and I thought I saw Mama breathe a sigh of relief. She wouldn't want Lillie to make a scene in front of important visitors from up north.

"Well, Charlie," Dr. Livingston said. "Is that a yes? Of course you can bring whoever you like along, and we'll even pay your first mate $1 a day."

Now I really lit up. Tiger would be so excited! I'd landed him a job!

But I tried not to let the excitement show on my face. "Well," I said carefully, "let me talk to Tiger, and if everything you say is true, then I think we have a deal, Dr. Livingston."

"Excellent!" he said, standing up. "Now, where can I find a decent hotel around here?"

"Hotel?" Mama said, looking flustered and a little embarrassed. "Oh, dear. There isn't a hotel within 100 miles of here." Then she quickly covered up with a smile. "But of course you can stay here. Why, we'd love to have you as our guests!"

Dr. Livingston accepted the invitation graciously…while I was already starting to plan another trip deep into Pa-Hay-Okee.

Chapter Three

Lillie Pulls a Fast One

I was up early the next morning, planning on heading north to find Tiger. But I stopped in surprise when I walked into the kitchen and found Mama mixing up pancake batter, with Lillie sitting at the table watching her.

"Pancakes?" I said. "It's not Sunday, is it?"

"No, no," Mama said. "I just thought we'd give our guests a decent breakfast when they get up."

"Pancakes?" I said again, dumbfounded. I'd never in my life seen Mama make pancakes on a weekday morning. "Where's Papa?"

"He's already out," Mama said. "You know him. Up with the dawn."

"So," Lillie cut in, "what do you think about this Dr. Livingston?"

"I think $5 a day is a lot of money, that's what I think," I said.

Lillie smirked, and I saw Mama roll her eyes.

"Why are you smirking?" I said to Lillie.

"You really think he's going to pay you $5 a day to take him on a boat ride?" said Lillie. "No way, I say. I bet he's a swindler."

Now it was my turn to roll my eyes. "Why would anybody swindle me? Anyway, if you don't believe he is who he says, why don't you ask him? See if he knows anything about plants after all."

"Fine," Lillie said. "I will."

"Children," Mama said sternly, looking up from her mixing bowl. "Dr. Livingston is a guest here. I won't have you interrogating him."

"Oh, Mama," Lillie said sweetly. "No one's going to interrogate him. I'm just gonna ask him a few questions."

I didn't stay to eat, but instead headed out into the early morning and up to the lake. Just as I hoped, I found Tiger and his father camping among the dunes that ran along the barrier islands. I told Tiger about the job. Just like Lillie, Tiger was suspicious at first—he thought Dr. Livingston might be a plume hunter. But when I told him the professor was a naturalist who just wanted to collect a few plants, he shrugged. "White people," he said, shaking his head.

"And get this," I told him. "He'll pay you $1 per day if you agree to come along. Not too bad, eh? What do you say?"

Now Tiger looked excited, and even his dad looked up from where he'd been stirring the fire.

"You go," he said.

When Tiger and I got back home, Dr. Livingston was sitting on our porch looking comfortable and reading a thick book. Mr. Bartley sat next to him, scratching in some kind of journal. They both looked up at Tiger like he was an ostrich. I guess they'd never seen a Seminole before.

"So," I said, after introducing Tiger as my first mate, "all that's left is the matter of the boat. I've been thinking about that, and I've got a few ideas. We'll need a ship that's big enough to handle sailing the coast some seventy miles down to Bis-cayne Bay, then across Florida Bay and around Cape Sable. We'll go up the Shark River and from there—"

"Into Pa-Hay-Okee," Tiger finished, smiling.

"Right," I said, grinning back at my friend.

"We'll be sailing through Ponce de León Bay, won't we?" Dr. Livingston asked. "Forgive me for not knowing the geography as well as you, but it's the only name I recognize. He was a very important explorer."

"Sure we will," I said, feeling good because I knew something this professor from Yale didn't. "That's just to the north of Cape Sable, where the Shark River is."

The professor sighed happily. "Imagine! Sailing through the same waters as Ponce de León!"

Tiger and I shot each other a look. By the time we got there, I figured the professor would have a whole different opinion of Ponce de León Bay and even Pa-Hay-Okee itself. That place was just about as far away from Yale University as you could get, especially in the summer. Papa sometimes joked that the mosquitoes were so bad in the summer, they could carry away a full-grown man.

"Anyway," I said, "about this boat. As long as my Papa agrees, I think I know just how to —"

Before I could finish telling him my idea, Lillie sauntered out onto the porch with both Mama and Papa following her.

Uh-oh, I thought. Here it comes.

But then Lillie curtsied to the professor, who acknowledged her with a nod. I'd never seen Lillie curtsy unless Mama was standing right behind her holding a wooden spoon.

"Professor?" she asked in her sweetest voice.

"Yes?" he responded.

She glanced at Mama before giving the professor a smile. I wondered who had replaced my sister with this strange girl.

"My mama said I had to ask your permission to come along on your plant expedition," she said.

"What?" I said, and Tiger let out a short laugh. "Lillie ain't coming along!"

Lillie shot me a dirty look. "I'm not asking you, Charlie. It ain't—"

"Isn't, dear. It isn't," Mama said.

"It isn't your expedition," Lillie finished with a satisfied look on her face. "It's the professor's here. He's the one paying for it, so I'm asking him."

"But—"

"Charlie!" Papa said, cutting me off.

I was confused, but also annoyed. It wasn't that I didn't like Lillie—of course I did. She was my sister. But what self-respecting big brother wants his little sister tagging along on every adventure? Even if she was better in the woods than me.

"What about her studies?" I asked.

"Well, that's just it," Lillie said. "The professor here and Mr. Bartley are preeminent naturalists."

Preeminent? I almost gagged. Just that morning, Lillie had been trying to convince me Dr. Livingston was a swindler, and now he was a preeminent naturalist? I got the feeling this was something she'd cooked up. She had that look about her, like I was falling into a trap.

29

Mr. Bartley looked uncomfortable too and said, "Most people just call me Bartley. I'm not that old."

Lillie smiled and continued, "And how many girls get the chance to travel with and learn from the world's best naturalist?"

And there it was. All of a sudden I saw what was happening. I could tell from Mama's expression that she had agreed to this tom-fool plan, and I could guess why.

Here's one thing I knew about Mama: she cared about our schooling, especially Lillie's, more than almost anything else. Where she was from, up in Chicago, Mama had gone to a school where girls learned proper etiquette as well as history and geography, diction and elocution. I guess at that school, Mama had picked up what Papa once called "peculiar ideas" about education for girls. She said that girls should get every bit as much schooling as boys. As a result, ever since Lillie had run away from her fancy girl's school, Mama had been schooling Lillie herself every day.

But I also knew that Mama was reaching the end of her tolerance…and the end of her library. They'd read most every book we had so many times that the words were almost worn off them. Lillie must have convinced Mama that our trip would be some kind of floating school.

"Well," said a clearly pleased Dr. Livingston, looking at Lillie, "the best naturalist in the world? That is a fine compliment, Miss Lillie, but even I can't lay claim to being the world's greatest scientist. That title must surely belong to Mr. Charles Darwin. Do you like science, Miss Lillie?"

"If by science you mean things that fly and crawl and swim, I reckon I like it more than Charlie does. Won't you please let me come? I promise I'll be good, and I'll even handle the cooking and help Charlie with the chores."

"Cooking?" I said, astounded. Lillie couldn't cook to save her life. That girl could burn water.

"Cooking indeed," said Dr. Livingston. "If your cooking is anywhere near as good as your mama's, then you'll be welcome on any boat I'm on." He turned to me and said, "Now Charlie, about this boat? What do you think?"

"Uh, I don't know quite yet," I stammered, still shocked at this turn of events. "I'll have to figure it out."

"You go ahead and do that then," he said, "and the sooner the better. We're anxious to get underway. Until then, I'll surely be looking forward to more of your mama's splendid cooking."

Chapter Four

The *Creole*

It didn't take long before Papa and I felt like interlopers in our own house. Dr. Livingston sure did know how to make himself at home, and as far as I could tell, looking after yourself was not included in the job description of a professor at Yale. Mama was cooking three large meals every day, and before I knew it, she was even doing their laundry.

Bartley either had his nose stuck in a book all the time, or was writing in his journal, while Dr. Livingston kept up a stream of flattery directed at Mama that would make a lobster blush. At the same time, Lillie kept up a stream of questions about plants and animals that I think even exhausted the poor professor. Turned out he was a real naturalist, though, because that man knew more about plants than anyone I'd ever met.

While all this was going on, I kept myself busy designing the perfect boat for our expedition. It was an exciting prospect. The year before, we'd learned a few things when we had to abandon our little boat because the water got too shallow. This time, I was envisioning a flat-bottom skiff with a shallow keel that skimmed across the surface and hardly drew any water at all, but was still big enough and sturdy enough to handle sailing on the open ocean.

As it happened, I thought I knew how to get exactly such a boat—as long as Papa agreed to my plan.

A few months before Dr. Livingston arrived, word had gone through the lake country that a ship had wrecked on the beach not too far north. Shipwrecks were always exciting because you never knew what goods they'd be selling or what you could scavenge from the beach. It might be anything from fresh-spun cotton meant for England to sugar or lumber.

This most recent shipwreck was called the *Providencia*, and I'd seen it with Papa just after it wrecked. She was a big Spanish ship that her captain had run aground, and two friends of Papa's named Mr. Hammon and Mr. Lanehart had gotten the salvage rights to the ship. Pretty soon they were selling supplies from the *Providencia* up and down the coast. This included about twenty thousand coconuts from the island of Trinidad, which they were selling for two and one-half cents apiece.

Papa bought himself two hundred of the coconuts and planted them on our island. Papa also bought and gave two hundred coconuts to Cecil Upton and seven hundred more to Captain Armour up at the lighthouse, and each man planted his land full of coconut trees. Cap Dimick also bought coconuts and planted them all over the barrier island near his homestead.

Later, when it came time to name our area, they picked a name that fit a place full of graceful coconut palms. They called it Palm Beach.

I wasn't so interested in the coconuts, but Papa's generosity with the coconuts paid off in another way. When Mr. Lanehart and Mr. Hammon saw Papa giving away so many coconuts to the other settlers who could not afford them, they gave him the *Providencia's* old longboat for free. Papa had taken it, but we hadn't really needed it, so he'd put it up on blocks on the island. That is, we hadn't needed it until I nervously explained my idea to Papa.

"Hmm," he said, looking at the weather-beaten longboat. "That just might work, Charlie."

Papa was the kind of man who liked to make things, and I think he was excited by my idea too. It didn't hurt that it would keep him out of the house while he helped me build it.

We started right away. The longboat had a flat bottom but no keel, so we knocked a hole in the bottom and rigged it with a special centerboard we could raise up in shallow water. Then we covered the bow with decking and built a small cabin on top of that. Finally, we rigged it with a small mast and hung a jib and mainsail. When we were done, we had a sturdy little ship of twenty-seven feet with an eight-foot beam and plenty of room to lash a little canoe to the stern.

I was plenty proud of her. We'd created a true combination oceangoing and shallow-draft swamp sailing boat, the first I'd ever heard of. Because she had been Spanish and was now American, we called her the *Creole*.

When we were done, Dr. Livingston looked over the *Creole*, thumping her hull a few times like a doctor, and announced that he was pleased with her. He immediately declared that he and Bartley could sleep in the cabin and suggested that, since we had grown up in Florida, me, Lillie, and Tiger could sleep under the stars on the deck. I reminded myself to get some mosquito netting.

Over the next few days, we loaded the *Creole* with everything we'd need. We took some salt and flour, some hard tack and dried venison, plus plenty of supplies like rope, fishhooks and cast nets, cooking gear, blankets, and powder for my rifle.

After we had packed the essentials, Bartley and Dr. Livingston brought aboard their gear. One item in particular caught my attention. It was an empty case made completely of glass with a peaked roof, like a Seminole chickee hut, and a tiny door in its side.

"Be careful with that!" Bartley said when I picked the case up to carry it onboard. "It's very fragile!"

"What is it?" I asked. "Looks like a house for leprechauns."

Tiger laughed, but Bartley looked annoyed.

"It's not a house for leprechauns," he said. "It's called a Wardian case. It's for protecting plant specimens and keeping them alive."

"You're going to put plants in there?" I asked, peering into the empty case.

"That's exactly what we're going to do," he said. "Now please, it's very fragile and very expensive."

I put the Wardian case belowdeck in the cabin, figuring that if Bartley was so worried about it, he'd want to keep it close at hand.

On the morning we were to leave, I was up before dawn, worrying that we might have forgotten something and worrying even more that I would be a good guide and leader. The house was still quiet, so I jumped a little when a soft knock sounded at my door. The door opened and Mama stuck her head in.

"I heard you were up," she said. "Can I come in?"

"Sure."

She sat down on my bed while I stuffed clothes into my bag.

"Charlie?" she finally said.

"Yes, Mama?"

She frowned a little and looked worried. "You'll take care of Lillie out there, right?"

I stopped packing and looked at her.

"I'm just saying," she said, "I know Lillie was born to these woods like a fish to the water. I do know that. And I know she's fearsomely stubborn when she wants to be. But, well, she's still a young girl. You understand, Charlie. You'll watch out for her?"

I laughed and took Mama's hand. "You don't have to worry about Lillie, Mama," I said. "She'll have me and Tiger there, and anyway, just ask her. She's better'n me in the swamps anyway."

Mama smiled thinly. "I know, I know. But a mother can worry, can't she?"

"She'll be fine. We all will be. And when we come back, I hope you like violin music, because you'll be hearing plenty of it."

Now Mama smiled for real. "I love it, Charlie. I can't wait to hear you play."

Chapter Five

Name That Plant

We finally shoved off on a bright summer morning with the heat rising like steam from the water. Black rain clouds rode the distant western horizon, and it was just a matter of time until the regular rains would start.

You never knew when the rains were going to start. You couldn't set a calendar by it, and no almanac predicted them. But when they started, it would rain every day in big warm drops that filled up all the lakes and rivers.

Mama and Papa came down to the dock to help us cast off lines. Just as we left the dock and Mama was waving and calling, "Be safe now!" Lillie's pet raccoon, Bandit, appeared, as if from nowhere, and jumped onto the boat. Lillie and Tiger laughed as Bandit stood on his back legs, with his paws up on the gunwale, and watched the dock slip away.

Those first few days were easy traveling. We stuck to the coast and sailed south for Biscayne Bay. The first night, we dropped anchor at the Lake Boca Raton Inlet, and the professor explained that Boca Raton meant "mouth of the rat" in Spanish because that's how the lake looked on a map when the Spanish first discovered it.

We made it to the top of Biscayne Bay the second night, and by the third night, we were at the mouth of the Miami River. I remembered this place from the year before and was surprised how much the area had changed. Brickell's trading post was bigger, and there were boats sailing on the bay. They were either coming or going from Miami, which I guess was turning into a proper town.

The hardest part of these early days was not falling asleep from boredom, at least for Tiger and me. It turned out that Bartley and Dr. Livingston had no interest in fishing for snook or even shark, or in spearing any of the fish that swam by in the clear waters. Every time I hinted that we should stop and throw out a line, Dr. Livingston would say something like, "I say we press on!" And since I was the guide, I had no choice but to agree — no matter how sad Tiger looked about it.

If that wasn't bad enough, Dr. Livingston soon invented the single most boring game I'd ever heard of. It even had a boring name. He called it Name That Plant.

Dr. Livingston would point at some patch of trees along the shore and say, "What's that?"

Then Bartley would say something like, "Sea grape."

And Dr. Livingston would say, "In Latin. Quick."

And Bartley would say, *"Coccoloba uvifera."*

Then they'd go on to the next one. "Those trees there… quick."

"Gumbo-limbo," Bartley would say. *"Bursera simaruba."*

I made the mistake once of asking why every plant needed two names when one name was good enough for me. This got me a long explanation from both Bartley and Dr. Livingston about exactly why plants have a two-word Latin name, one for the genus and one for the species. They said it was so people could keep them all straight.

When I pointed out that it still seemed confusing, Dr. Livingston turned to Tiger and asked, "What do your people call that tree there?" He pointed onshore to the little cabbage palms.

"Tah-lah-kul-kluk-ka," Tiger replied.

"Right," Dr. Livingston said. "Now, Charlie, let's say you wanted to find some of those and the only person you could ask was a Seminole. You'd have no idea! But now imagine if everyone used the same word. Then everybody who wanted to identify those trees would be able to understand each other."

"If you say so," I said, thinking that I was definitely earning my $5 today.

Then Lillie piped up excitedly, "I get it. That way, it doesn't matter what language you're using."

"Exactly, Miss Lillie," Dr. Livingston said, smiling and looking more pleased than ever. "Latin is the universal language of science."

From that moment on, Lillie played along with Name that Plant while I sailed the boat and Tiger pretended to throw his spear at any nearby fish just to keep himself occupied.

On the fourth day—what I privately called my "Twenty Dollar Day" because that's how much I'd already earned—we made the 15-mile trip to Black Point. I was worried we'd get stuck in the mud flats again, just like we had last year, but we crossed at high tide and I was pleased to see that the *Creole* skimmed across the water just like I'd hoped she would.

When we sailed into Card Sound, it was just like I remembered: water so clear it looked like air and thick with fish. Finally, near sunset, Tiger couldn't stand it any longer and speared a redfish the size of his arm. I heard him whooping in excitement and turned to see him go over the side after his fish.

"That's quite a fish," Dr. Livingston said when Tiger climbed back on deck with the giant fish dangling from his spear. "Quite a fish."

Unfortunately, we weren't the only ones on board who liked Tiger's fish. Bandit popped up as soon as Tiger started cleaning the fish. His whiskers were twitching and his little paws itching to steal our dinner. Tiger threw him a few bits, but that only seemed to make the little raccoon hungrier, and pretty soon he had swiped almost half the fish, including the tender tail meat. We all laughed as Tiger chased Bandit around the boat, yelling at him in Seminole to give back his fish.

Still, there was plenty left over for an excellent fish stew that night.

"Tiger," I said, my mouth full of fish. "Where'd you learn how to cook like this?"

He shrugged, but I could tell he was proud. From then on, Tiger did the cooking.

The next day, Dr. Livingston and Bartley spent all day hanging over the edge of the boat, watching the parade of colorful fish, coral, and sea fans slide below us. Dr. Livingston said he'd seen coral in the Pacific Ocean, the Indian Ocean, and in the Caribbean, but he'd never seen any place so beautiful as Card Sound.

But I wasn't paying attention to coral. The whole time we were sailing through Florida Bay, I kept an eye on the black clouds hanging over Pa-Hay-Okee. I'd seen the summer rain clouds my whole life, but for some reason, these heavy black clouds seemed ominous. I didn't mention this feeling to anyone else, especially Dr. Livingston or Bartley. I figured that people from Yale wouldn't put much stock in a sailor's superstitions, and the last thing I wanted

was to look foolish. I was the guide, after all. I had to act like it.

Finally, on the sixth day after we left the lake country, we sailed around Cape Sable and into Ponce de León Bay and crossed a line in the water where the dark runoff from Pa-Hay-Okee tangled with the clear, green water of the bay. As the *Creole* slid into this murky water, the others clustered at the edge to watch. Overhead, great flocks of birds wheeled against the bright sky and dove into the murk for minnows. A pod of dolphins nearby worked the dirty waterline, chasing baitfish until they leapt from the water like silver bolts of light.

I was at the rudder when Dr. Livingston came back to stand next to me. "I wonder," he said in a quiet voice, watching the birds do their work, "I wonder if the great man himself sailed through this bay."

"Great man?" I said.

"Ponce de León," Dr. Livingston said. "The man who discovered Florida."

I shrugged. "I expect so. He got the bay named after him, after all."

"Yes, I expect he did." Then Dr. Livingston looked at the heavy black clouds sweeping across Pa-Hay-Okee, trailing their streamers of rain. "Did you know de León was killed here?" he asked. "Technically, he died in Cuba. But the arrow that caused the fatal injury was shot in the wilds of South Florida by a band of natives." He paused. "You're worried, aren't you, Charlie?"

I glanced at him. "Not too bad," I said. "We just need to be careful, that's all."

"But it's a dangerous place, this Pa-Hay-Okee," he said. "A dangerous place indeed."

I glanced over at him, not sure what he meant by this.

"I reckon it can be," I said. "But down here, every place is dangerous. It's like my Papa says, there's no telling."

"No," said Dr. Livingston. "I guess not."

Chapter Six

Bartley Finds an Orchid

We spent that night far up the Shark River, anchored in the middle of the river and swatting at bugs. Even with mosquito nets draped over the deck, I must have got bit a hundred times from the swarms of buzzing mosquitoes.

Sometime in the middle of the night, it rained hard, which brought Dr. Livingston and Bartley to the door of the cabin to watch it come down.

I don't know what rain is like in other places, but from the way Dr. Livingston and Bartley acted, I guessed they'd never seen rain like this before. It didn't come riding on a thunderstorm but instead in a flat sheet that swept over the sawgrass and the *Creole* like a drum roll. It rained in giant warm drops that soaked me to the bone and sent little rivers coursing down our deck. I didn't much like being wet, but I sure didn't mind that the rain drove the mosquitoes away.

Then all of a sudden, the rain stopped and the moon came out. The professor and Bartley went back to bed, and a few minutes later I smelled cherry pipe smoke from below and saw the faint glow of a lantern. I knew Dr. Livingston wasn't sleeping either, but I had no idea why he needed a light in the middle of the night.

Far off in the swamp, some great animal bellowed.

"Charlie?" Lillie whispered from under her net.

"Yeah?"

"I'm wet and cold."

"Me too."

"What was that noise?"

"I dunno," I said. "Some animal, I guess. Maybe a bear."

"That weren't no bear," she said.

"Wasn't any bear," I said automatically.

"Oh please," Lillie said. "Not you too." She was quiet for a second, then she said, "Don't you have a weird feeling about this trip?"

I shrugged. "No, not really."

"Huh," she said. "I like Dr. Livingston. He knows more about science than anyone I ever met. But there's something about him that don't feel right to me."

"Hush," I said. "He's awake down there. Anyway, I figure we won't be out here for long. I'm sure Dr. Livingston doesn't want to pay me to sail him all over the swamp for too long, especially with all this rain and the mosquitoes. And it seems to me like there's plants all over the place. The way I see it, we'll spend a few days and stuff that case of Bartley's full of plants, then head home. We'll be home in ten days. Mark my words."

"Yeah," she said. "I reckon you're right."

I heard her rustle under her net, pulling her thin blanket around her. "G'night, Charlie."

"G'night."

It dawned hot and bright, with scores of birds fluttering up from the rain-soaked grass to swoop and dive through the clouds of bugs. Good for you, I thought. Fill up your bellies because the more you eat, the less there'll be to bother me.

For breakfast, Tiger made us a quick meal of fresh eggs scrambled with some kind of small fish that we ate whole, plus a few lumps of cured pork belly. The whole time Tiger was cooking, Bandit was trying to get his paws on one of the eggs, but Tiger shooed him away. When I asked Tiger where he got the eggs, he just grinned to himself. I guess he wanted to keep it a mystery.

There wasn't good wind this deep in the swamp, so after breakfast we broke out the long poles and pushed the *Creole* against the gentle current. A few hours in, the centerboard started hitting bottom, so we pulled it up partway and wedged it in position. I was proud to see that it didn't leak water. Our design worked.

It wasn't until lunch that we finally found a hammock close enough and dry enough to wade ashore. We dropped anchor, and the five of us were soon in waist-deep water, pushing toward the shore. Even from a distance, I could hear the thousands of insects in the trees and the squawk of birds.

It was strange, though, because there weren't nearly as many birds as I remembered from our last trip. When I mentioned this to Tiger, it was Bartley who answered.

"They're migratory," he said. "Most of them leave in the summer and fly north. They only come down in the winter to mate. We even get egret in Connecticut."

"Oh," I said, feeling annoyed that it took a student from Yale to tell me something about the place where I lived. But Bartley wasn't done yet.

"This is a hammock," he went on, his eyes gleaming while he looked ahead at the low island. "See those trees and vines? It's like a little jungle stuck here in the middle of the swamp. There's ficus there. Wild cinnamon trees. Cassia. All kinds of plants you'd normally find in the tropics."

"And orchids, right?" I offered helpfully.

"And orchids," he said.

50

We waded onshore a few minutes later, and Bartley rushed forward, heading for a scrubby tree near the shoreline that looked like it had grown a beard. We all followed him and gathered around as he and Dr. Livingston inspected a mass of flowers.

"What is it?" Dr. Livingston asked his pupil.

"Don't know, Professor," Bartley answered promptly, his eyes gleaming. "Maybe it's new."

I didn't see what was so exciting about it until I looked closely at the plant. It was maybe the first time in my life I'd ever looked really closely at a flower, and even I began to see what had captured Bartley's imagination. The orchid grew stuck to the side of the tree, its thick stems clinging to the tree like a possum to a branch. Its leaves weren't much to speak of, just light green spears sticking up from the stems, but it had masses of colorful flowers that, when I looked close, were pale green, like eel skin, with brown freckles and a bright yellow throat surrounded by red. It was hard to believe any flower so small could be so pretty, or that I'd spent my whole life surrounded by these things and never even noticed. Why, if Mama had looked closely at one of these, I'm sure she would have decorated the whole house with bunches of them.

"It's an epiphyte," Bartley said, producing a small knife from his belt and beginning to work on the trunk. "See? These are its roots."

Lillie craned to see while Bartley scraped away thin grey filaments from the tree trunk. They didn't look like any roots I'd ever seen.

"So how does it grow?" Lillie asked. "If its roots don't go into the ground like a normal plant? How does it get water?"

"It takes moisture and nutrients right from the rainwater and from leaves that fall into the plant. That's what makes them so special. See these roots? They're grey because it rained last night and they're full of water. When they dry out, they'll turn silvery white."

Bartley was careful to cut away a small portion of the orchid with its roots intact, leaving the rest of the plant alone. Then he wrapped it in a wad of wet moss he pulled from the scraggly little tree and set it inside his glass case. When he was done, he immediately hurried off, deeper into the damp shadows under the trees.

Lillie and I shrugged at each other and followed, while Dr. Livingston headed off along the shore to find more plants on his own.

As far as I could tell, this would be the easiest money anybody'd ever made. It looked like there were enough plants on this one hammock to stuff Bartley's whole case full and then some. Maybe he'd even find one of those ghost orchids they were looking for.

As I ran to catch up to Bartley, I looked over my shoulder to see Tiger down by the water's edge, digging around with a long branch. Whatever he was looking for, I hoped it was tasty.

Chapter Seven

The Ancient Village

Over the next two days, we visited many such hammocks, and Bartley stuffed his little glass house nearly full of orchids. Along the way, he taught Lillie all kinds of Latin names for flowers and plants, and before long she was *Oncidium*-ing and *Prosthechea*-ing with the best of them.

I wasn't surprised when it turned out that Lillie had the best eye for spotting flowers, better even than Dr. Livingston or Bartley. More than a few times, Bartley sent her scampering up a tall cypress or bay tree, with Bandit climbing up after her, to bring down some tiny plant decorated with flowers like jewels.

In the evenings, after a day of collecting flowers, Bartley sat on deck making drawings of all the new flowers and labeling their parts. When Lillie asked him why he was bothering to draw a plant he had sitting right in front of him, he explained that's how scientists share new plants with other scientists.

"What do you mean 'new plants'?" Lillie asked. "These aren't new. They've been here forever."

"I mean new to science," Bartley said, and then he was off talking again, explaining how the world was topped to the gills with plants and animals that scientists had never heard of, and it was up to explorers to find them, draw them, give them names, and study them so we could learn how the world really worked.

Lillie was all ears, and I swear it even looked like Bandit was paying attention too.

While all this was going on, Tiger and I kept ourselves busy catching food. I had my rifle, of course, and we both had fishing line and hooks. We caught little mosquito fish by the basketful near the surface, and I landed a bass almost as long my forearm. Pretty soon, Tiger evened the score with a big turtle he caught by hand off a floating log. That night, he roasted the bass on a sapling spit over a fire and made a delicious turtle stew.

The whole trip was turning out pretty well, I thought, and my Dollar Day clock was running strong. I was already almost up to $50 and we were still pushing deeper into the swamp. It turned out Dr. Livingston was set on finding this ghost orchid. At every new hammock, he'd only wade ashore for a minute or two, glance around the trees, and then shake his head. "Not here," he'd declare, and then he'd head back to the *Creole* and let Lillie and Bartley spend the next three hours scraping plants off tree trunks while Tiger and I took turns shooting at or fishing for our next meal.

More than once I saw Dr. Livingston refer to

a little brown book. I guess it was his own version of Bartley's plant journal.

While Dr. Livingston fretted about his precious ghost orchid, I kept us pushing deeper into the swamp. Gradually, the open sawgrass and hammocks started to give way to cypress trees and narrow, choked streams with cypress knees sticking up like bones in a flooded boneyard.

One evening, while Tiger was cooking up a possum I'd shot earlier that day, Dr. Livingston came back to the rudder stick, next to me. He sat down on the gunwale. I had a fishing line in the water, but it was more for something to do than anything else because I couldn't stand listening to Lillie and Bartley anymore.

"So Charlie," Dr. Livingston started, rubbing his beard. He'd browned up in the hot sun and looked almost like a real Floridian. "I wanted to have a word with you, if I may."

"Sure," I said, twitching on my pole a little bit to make the bait bounce.

"When I first learned about you, I heard you'd taken your group to a wild place deep in the swamp."

"Yep, I reckon that's true," I said. "It wasn't just me, though. We all went together."

"Yes," he said, looking down into the brown-tinged water at the little fish circling my bait. "What was it like there, Charlie? Were there many islands? Like a cluster of islands?"

I thought about it. "Well, I reckon there were a lot of islands around there, but there are a lot of islands throughout this area. Are you looking for a special island?"

"Here's my thinking, Charlie. Man to man. We'll have better luck with this ghost orchid the more islands we find. So I was hoping you knew of a place that is positively thick with islands, a place where they are clustered as close together as seeds on a sunflower head."

"Well…" I stalled, trying to figure out what he was driving at. "There was a place as isolated and wild as any in the world. And there were a fair number of islands there, with big cypress forests. Is that the kind of place you mean?"

"Perhaps," he said. "Because I've begun to worry, Charlie, that the ecosystem in these hammocks isn't the right one for what I'm searching for. Orchids are very specific. They only grow in particular places, each to its own place. And I'm afraid we're in the wrong place. Which direction is this place you're describing?"

"North of here. Less than a day's travel away."

"I see, I see," he said.

Then I thought of something. "Just one thing," I said. "It's not easy traveling, Dr. Livingston. Even in the high water, we're just about as shallow as the *Creole* can go. I figure tomorrow, we're going to have to tie up and wade in the rest of the way. We can pile up some provisions in our little canoe, but it'll be wet and dirty travel."

Dr. Livingston looked up and smiled. "I'm an explorer, Charlie. Wet and dirty travel comes with the territory. You just lead us onward, young man, and I'm sure we'll get there."

The next morning, we threaded our way up a winding stream through the cypress until about mealtime, when the centerboard was hitting so many downed trees underwater that I was afraid it would snap off and leave us stranded. I announced it was time to stop, eat, and pile whatever basics we needed into the small dugout canoe we'd lashed to the back of the *Creole*.

"We'll walk from here," I said.

No one complained, but I thought Bartley looked a little nervous and mumbled something about gators. I'll admit the prospect of stepping on a gator didn't excite me either, but only because I didn't cherish the thought of getting knocked over. Unless they're breeding, gators always run at the sight of a person. Almost always.

After we ate, we slipped into the warm brown water and started wading. Tiger tied the little canoe full of supplies to his arm with a short rope so it bobbed along after us. Bandit made himself comfortable sitting on top of our supplies and chattering away at the birds and passing trees.

After several hours of soggy wading, the land

under our feet began to rise. Surrounded by clouds of mosquitoes, we waded out of the water and stood dripping on dry land. I couldn't be sure, but I was pretty sure I'd led us back to the old abandoned village we had stumbled on last year. We pulled the canoe onto shore and pushed forward.

It was cooler and dim under the high tree branches, even though it was still midday. Only occasional beams of sunlight lanced down to the ground, mixing in with the wild creepers and moon vines, the cypress and the hardwood trees. Overhead, masses of plants were bunched up in the tree branches, many with flowers hanging from them.

Before long, Dr. Livingston had taken the lead. I'd never seen him so excited before, and he walked with strides so long Lillie almost had to jog to keep up with him.

I kept expecting him to yell out, "There it is!" and point to a pale white flower hanging from a rough tree trunk high overhead.

Instead, we soon came to the steep, short hill I remembered, and Tiger and I exchanged a glance. We'd made it back to the abandoned village. Last year, we'd come here just before finding the snowy egret island across another stretch of sawgrass. I'd remembered the place was thick with flowers and plants, just the place to bring orchid hunters.

We clambered up the gentle slope, and sure enough, both Bartley and Dr. Livingston stopped short in shock. Underneath the branches, there were huge shell piles scattered on the forest floor and stone rings atop raised mounds. The ground was dusty and hard-packed.

"What is this place?" Dr. Livingston breathed.

"I don't know," I said. "Some kind of ancient abandoned village, I guess."

"Indian?" Dr. Livingston said.

"Not Seminole," Tiger said. "Older."

We spread out and walked into the deserted village. There were no huts or homes, just the tall mounds of shells and small raised hills where buildings must have once stood. The place still had the same haunted feeling I remembered, like we were being watched by something old and invisible.

I glanced over to see Lillie and Bandit following along behind Bartley, and Tiger squatting next to a ring of stones. Dr. Livingston was at the far edge of the clearing, kneeling over and closely inspecting one of the shell mounds. While I watched, he swept away a small pile of shells and got so close to the ground I thought he was sniffing it.

I walked over to Tiger and squatted next to him. Just like I'd thought, he was sifting through ashes in one of the fire rings.

"What you looking at?" I asked. "You see something to eat in there?"

"Strange," Tiger said. "Remember last year? Ashes were fresh, like someone was just here. These are new too. But not so new. Maybe months old."

"Huh," I grunted. "Maybe forest fire?"

Tiger glanced at me. "No. People fire."

"But there aren't any people around here."

"There were," he said. "Last winter. Must be winter camp."

"Are you sure they're not Seminoles?" I said.

Tiger shook his head. "No. Not Seminole."

"Then who?"

"Don't know."

I'd heard stories, of course, of fugitives living in the swamp. Everyone in Florida had heard of them. Runaway Confederate soldiers from the War Between the States. Old slaves who hadn't heard about emancipation. Criminals. Even Seminoles who had run into trouble with the law.

That thought gave me pause. I had no problem with any man wanting to live out his days in the great loneliness of this place—as long as he didn't have any problem with us. But I didn't want to run into any fugitives or dangerous people out here.

Tiger and I were still squatting by the cold

61

ashes when I heard Lillie's voice, "Charlie! Charlie! Quick!"

I jumped up, afraid of what I might see coming through the woods toward us. My sister didn't scare easy, and she sounded upset. But there was no one, except for Bartley standing on the edge of the clearing where Dr. Livingston had been just minutes before, and my sister scrambling over the mounds toward me.

"What is it?" I asked. "What are you hollering about?"

"It's Dr. Livingston!" she said. "He's gone, Charlie! He's gone!"

Just then, I heard Bartley's voice echoing through the big, dark trees.

"Dr. Livingston! Professor! Dr. Livingston!"

But there was no response.

I took off on a dead run for the edge of the clearing with Tiger two steps behind me.

Chapter Eight

North by Northwest

Running into the center of the clearing, I saw Lillie and Bandit heading one way and Bartley another way. I ran after Lillie. Mama's words were ringing in my head: "Watch out for your sister, Charlie."

If anything happened to Lillie, I would never forgive myself.

"Lillie!" I hollered, sprinting between the shell piles and raised mounds and into the dark cypress trees on the other side of the village. "Lillie! Wait!"

"Dr. Livingston!" Bartley's voice echoed from somewhere to my left.

Lillie didn't stop running, and I saw a flash of blond hair up ahead. Tiger was nearby, also running through the woods.

For the first time since we'd started this trip, I was truly scared. Even though the ashes in that fire pit were old, they made me nervous.

What if Dr. Livingston had run into a swamp fugitive? What if there was more than one? And that wasn't even counting the water moccasins and alligators.

"Lillie!"

The cypress forest here had tall trees and a soft floor that muffled our footsteps. It sounded like my voice only made it a few feet into the trees before it dropped to the ground like a fallen branch. I wasn't even sure Lillie could hear me.

Up ahead, I saw the bright light of the tree line and my sister's shape framed against the light.

"LILLIE!" I yelled.

She must have heard me that time because she slowed and looked over her shoulder, then let me catch up to her. I was panting and sweating and my heart was pounding.

"Lillie…" I panted. "You…shouldn't…run…away…like…that."

"I'm fine, Charlie," she said. "I was looking for Dr. Livingston. And I'm not afraid of the woods. You know—"

She stopped as we neared the edge of the trees and stood in the shadowy border between the shade of the cypress forest and the bright sunlight of the afternoon. "Look, Charlie," she whispered. "It's Dr. Livingston."

The professor was standing down the shore, looking up and holding something up to his face with one hand. It glinted in the sun like polished copper. In his other hand, he had his little leather flower book out again.

Tiger caught up to us, and Dr. Livingston must have heard because he turned around and saw us stepping from the shadows into the sunlight. He folded the instrument in his hand, closed his flower book, and put both back into some inner pocket of his jacket, smiling at us.

"Why hello there!" he said cheerfully, and suddenly I felt like a fool for worrying. Tiger had me jumping at shadows because of that old fire pit back at the empty village.

"Hi, Dr. Livingston," I said, walking to meet him along the narrow beach. "We were looking for you."

"Time to go already?" he said. "Has Bartley cleaned the place out?"

"Um, no sir," I said. "Not yet. We were just worried I guess."

Dr. Livingston's smile grew a notch. "Thought perhaps I'd become alligator food, eh Charlie? Well, I do appreciate your concern. Wouldn't do at all to have your paying customer eaten, now would it?"

"No sir," I said. "Sure wouldn't."

"What was that thing in your hand?" Lillie blurted out.

"Lillie!" I said, worried that she was being rude.

But Dr. Livingston didn't seem to mind. I guess he'd been traveling with Lillie long enough to know her ways by now.

"It's a device I use to measure light, Miss Lillie," he said. "As I'm sure Bartley has explained in detail, each species of orchid grows in a very particular place with just so much light. They're like fussy eaters, if you know what I mean. So by measuring light, I can find out where the ghost orchid is most likely to live. Would you like to see the device? It's really quite ingenious."

"No, that's fine," I cut in, shooting Lillie a "don't be nosy" look. She frowned at me and stuck her tongue out.

"So then," Dr. Livingston said, looking into the forest behind us. "Where's Bartley? Is he with you also? This is a most fascinating island you've taken us to. Those shell mounds are extraordinary. I can think of several of my colleagues who would pay good money to see this place. I suspect these mounds are older than I thought at first. Perhaps much older."

As he talked, he headed back into the forest and we trailed along after him. Stepping back into the cool shade, I shot Lillie a look and felt a little foolish for letting my imagination run away with me.

Bartley found us halfway back to the abandoned village. He looked sheepish too, especially when Dr. Livingston slapped him on the back and said, "Fear not, young Jonathan! We'll still find plenty of flowers for you!"

It was late afternoon when we got back to the village, so we decided to camp for the night. We unloaded supplies from our canoe and hung a blanket from the trees to form a crude tent. Tiger, meanwhile, started a small fire on the ashes of the older fire and made a supper that included handfuls of greens he'd collected from under the trees mixed with some salt pork and a handful of beans. Throughout the meal, Dr. Livingston seemed the most joyful of any of us, and I suspected his light-sensing device had shown him something earlier.

"Charlie," he said after the meal was over and we were all leaning back against the trees, or, in Lillie's case, chasing Bandit around the tall mounds.

"Yes?" I said.

"I was thinking…I wasn't much help earlier in describing the kind of place I think we need to find."

I didn't answer because it would have been rude to agree.

"But now that I have some more information, I think I can give you a better idea. What we're looking for is a good cluster of islands with a good northern exposure. To do that, I'm thinking we should head north by northwest, not north like we originally agreed."

"Northwest?" I said.

"Yes," he said. "I wouldn't expect you to know these sorts of details, of course, but what we need is a good northern exposure. The strength of the sun depends on which way you're facing, because of the way the Earth rotates around the sun. So you see, if you stand in one place all day and face the four directions of the compass, you'll find the sun hits you with different intensities depending on which way you're facing. To the north, you'll be in shadow virtually all day. To the east, you'll have the gentle morning sun and the sun on your back in the afternoon. To the west, you'll have strong afternoon sun but no direct sun in the morning. And to the south, you'll have the strongest sun all day."

"Makes sense," I said.

"The orchids I'm looking for don't like strong sunlight, so a northern exposure is perfect. And according to my calculations, the best chances we'll have for the kind of place I'm talking about is to head northwest from here."

I wasn't sure I understood what he was talking about, and even Bartley looked a little confused. But I figured that Dr. Livingston was the professor from Yale, and I was just the guide.

"Well if that's what you want," I said, "northwest it is, deeper into the swamp. Just remember, pretty soon we'll be in new country, so there's no telling what we'll find there. I can't guarantee you'll find your cluster of islands, and if we go far enough, we'll end up in the Gulf of Mexico."

Dr. Livingston nodded. "Understood," he said gravely.

As night fell, the mosquitoes came out in force, and we didn't have proper mosquito nets. We spent the night huddled under our blankets, throwing wet wood on the fire every so often. The wood sputtered and sent up great clouds of smoke, which helped keep the worst of the mosquitoes away, but made it hard to draw a proper breath. We all woke up tired and cranky and had a cold meal.

After we ate, we set off wading again through the sawgrass. It was hard travel, worse than I remembered. The blades of grass tugged at our clothes, and if a blade rubbed up against skin, it was sure to leave a scrape. And even though the water was warm, the bottom here was deep muck that sucked at our feet, threatening to pull off our shoes and making it hard to lift our legs.

Within an hour of wrenching my feet out of the muck, the muscles in my legs were burning with exhaustion.

The only one of us who didn't look miserable was Bandit. He spent the afternoon either on Lillie's shoulder or swimming alongside us, his little nose and sharp eyes above the water.

We didn't talk much while we walked, always looking for shallow water and heading for a chain of islands in the distance. The only one of us who talked regularly was Tiger, who kept holding up his hand and hissing for us to stop.

"What is it?" I finally asked after he called for another halt. Tiger was listening with his head cocked to one side. A great blue heron flapped overhead, sending a shadow rippling over the water.

"Nothing," he grunted after a minute.

"If you're worried about animals, what good will it do to keep stopping like this?" I asked. "We'd be better off to keep moving."

Tiger just looked at me with his black eyes.

We reached the first little island after lunchtime. We were all hungry, sore, and soaked. But I didn't think we would have to wade too much more. We were at the head of a chain of islands that seemed to drip with orchids and epiphytes. I figured Bartley would soon have more flowers than he could even carry.

"Whew," Bartley said as we walked on the shore and stood shaking muck from our shoes. "Can't say I'm sorry to be on dry land again. But look at this place," he said, his eyes shining as he looked at the trees and their clothing of flowers. "There must be dozens of unknown species here!"

"Look, Charlie," Lillie piped up, "my hands are wrinkled like grapes." She held them out so I could see her puckered fingers.

"Yeah," I said. "Me too. We should eat here, I think. Okay, Dr. Livingston?"

"Sure, Charlie, sure," he said. But even the professor was looking wet and bedraggled, like he could use a cool bath and a comfortable place to sit.

"Okay then," I said, turning to pull the canoe onshore and get our supplies. While I unpacked and everyone else climbed to higher ground, Tiger split away and came to help me. "Thanks," I said, grateful for the help.

But Tiger looked over his shoulder, and then leaned in close. "Charlie," he said in a whisper, "I think something is following us."

"What?" I said. "What do you mean following us?"

"Hard to explain, but I feel it."

My first thought was of a fugitive, but I pushed that away. I had an overactive imagination because of that old village. "It's probably a bear or panther," I said. "Remember those panthers from last year, the ones that came at night?"

Tiger squinted. "Don't know. Maybe."

"Don't worry about it too much," I said. "I tell you, Tiger, I'm not going to miss wading around all day when this is over."

When Tiger didn't respond, I added, "Really, Tiger, there's no sense in worrying about it. If some animal is following us, it's probably hoping we'll drop food." I paused. "Oh, and I wouldn't mention anything to the others. No reason to get them all riled up."

Chapter Nine

A Deal with Bartley

By late that afternoon, I fervently wished Tiger had never said anything to me about being followed. All the rest of that day, as we waded toward another island in the distance, I was nervous and jumpy as a cat. Every time a bird flew overhead or fluttered up above the tall sawgrass, I started imagining all kinds of things, from ragged and bearded old outlaws creeping just behind us to a black bear or panther coming thrashing through the sawgrass.

"Charlie," Lillie said when we finally climbed onto another dry shore. "What's got into you?"

"Huh? Nothing," I said. "Nothing's got into me."

"Charlie Pierce," she said, and just then she sounded more like Mama than I'd ever heard. "I don't believe you for a second."

I saw Dr. Livingston watching me and felt foolish again. It was embarrassing to get caught arguing with my little sister in front of him and Bartley. "I don't care if you believe me, Lillie. Stop back-sassing me."

Lillie gave me a look like she hadn't heard me

right. "You're not Papa, Charlie. You can't talk to me like that."

"Lillie, just be quiet, would you?"

"You can't tell me what to do either!"

I could see she was getting madder, and I knew I better figure out some way to get out of this without a full-blown fight with Lillie. If she reminded me of Mama just then, I felt like Papa.

Fortunately, Bartley came to my rescue. "Look at this place," he said. "I like the look of this island, Professor. It must be stuffed to the gills with new species. What do you say, Lillie? You want to hunt for some flowers?"

Lillie instantly stopped paying any mind to me and said, "Sure!" She tagged after Bartley while he headed into the forest with Bandit trailing behind and shaking water from his fur. As they left, Bartley looked back over his shoulder and winked at me. I figured he must have a little sister too.

"Hmm," Dr. Livingston said. "If they're going that way, perhaps I'll head this way and we'll cover the island. Bartley is right, as usual, this is an excellent island. The sheer number of plants here is amazing." He headed off in the opposite direction, leaving me and Tiger on the beach.

"Whew," I said when we were alone. "I could use a minute to gather my thoughts."

Tiger was on the shore and looking over the water, his sharp eyes watching and reading the marsh in some language that most white people didn't understand.

"So you still think we're being followed?" I asked, standing next to him.

"Yes," Tiger said. "Watch."

The endless plain of sawgrass looked the same as always. Heat waves danced above the nodding sawgrass in the late afternoon sun, and a flock of birds startled up and flew into the air.

"There!" Tiger said, pointing. "Those birds. See?"

"Yeah. They're birds."

"But the way they all flew at once. Something scared them."

"I guess," I said. "But it could've been anything, Tiger. Even a needlenose fish. Birds scare easy."

He shook his head. "I don't think so. All day, same thing. Watch the animals. They say something is there. And Charlie, why would panther or bear follow us for whole day?"

"I told you," I said. "Because they're hungry. Try dropping a bit of bacon and see what happens to it."

"You funny, Charlie. Very funny."

Behind me, birds were calling in the thick hammock, and I could still hear Lillie laughing and chattering to Bartley as they headed into the heavy foliage. She sounded happy.

"Can I tell you something?" I said, lowering my voice. "I don't know where we're going at all. I have no idea where I'm supposed to be leading Dr. Livingston."

Tiger smiled, then started laughing.

"What's so funny?" I said. "I don't think that's very funny."

He pointed at me, then laughed some more until he slowed down and sputtered to a stop. "Oh, that funny, Charlie. Of course you lost! No one ever been here before."

"Is that your way of making me feel better?"

Tiger was still smiling when he laid a friendly hand on my shoulder. "You good guide, Charlie. Don't worry. Doctor and Bartley don't know where they going either."

That made me smile, and we began to set up camp for the night. I was looking forward to drying out. This island had white coral rocks on the beach that formed a natural shelf, and above that, dry land that would be good for a fire.

Tiger and I were just finishing setting up a

ring of stones for a fire when Lillie came out of the forest alone. I could hear Bartley in the trees behind her, and from the way she looked at me, I was afraid she was about to start up our fight again.

"I just saw Dr. Livingston," she said quickly. "He was using that device again."

"What?" I said, standing up and brushing my hands on my pants.

"We were in the trees and I heard something, so I went for a look and saw Dr. Livingston. He was down by the beach with that device again. And I saw his book, Charlie. He had it open. It's not like Bartley's flower book."

"So what if he was using his device?" I said. "It's a light thing or whatever."

She frowned. "I don't know," she said. "I think I've seen one of them before and it wasn't for light. And you know how Bartley's book is full of drawings of plants? Dr. Livingston's is a map book, Charlie. At least the part I saw. It's all maps!"

"Maps?" I said.

Just then, Bartley emerged from the trees lugging his Wardian case with even more plants stuffed in it. I couldn't believe how many orchids he'd stuffed in that case. Bartley was sweating from the close heat of the forest and mopping his face with his sleeve. He grinned at Lillie, but as soon as he saw us, the grin slipped from his face. "What?" he said. "Is everything okay?"

"Sure," I said.

"Why does Professor Livingston have a map book?" Lillie asked. "What do the maps show?"

"What?" Bartley asked. "What are you talking about?"

"Nothing," I said, anxious to stop Lillie from picking a fight with Bartley.

"What's Professor Livingston looking for on his maps?" Lillie asked.

"Maps? What maps?" Bartley said.

"In that book of his, the one he's always looking at. I saw it just now, when you were collecting that vanilla orchid. I saw Dr. Livingston, and he was standing by the shore with his light device again and his book open. I snuck up and got a look at his book, and it's a map book."

Bartley frowned. "What light device?"

"The one that tells how much light is in a place," Lillie said. "And maps."

"I don't know," Bartley said. "I've never seen a map before. And I don't know about any light device."

"Please, Lillie," I said. "You sound crazy. Dr. Livingston is paying us to guide him, not spy on him!"

"But I'm telling you, Charlie!" she said. "I don't trust him!"

From the way she clamped her mouth shut and looked immediately at Bartley, I could tell that she hadn't meant to go that far. But now that she'd said it, I could also tell she meant it. And Bartley didn't look very happy either. He just stood with his case, frowning at Lillie.

Now here's the thing about Lillie. She could be stubborn and even annoying sometimes. She didn't always do what little girls were supposed to do, and that included her ability to spit eight feet and hit an empty can every time. But I also knew Lillie was just about the smartest little sister ever, and I'd learned over the past few years that she was right about a lot of things.

I could tell her words had an effect on Tiger too. My friend was watching Lillie with very intense black eyes.

"Why don't you trust him, Lillie?" I said. "You must have a reason to say something like that."

Now it was her turn to frown, and she kicked at the sand. "That's just it, Charlie. I don't know exactly, but it's just my feeling. I bet if we could get a look at that book, it would tell us what he's up to."

"How we gonna do that?" I asked.

"I don't know," she said. "He's been hiding it from us so far, so he's not just going to let us wander over and peek through it. We need to figure out a way to get a look at it without him knowing."

"But that's his private property!" Bartley said. "I won't hear of this!"

I turned to Bartley. "I've seen this book too, Bartley, and he only looks at it when no one else is around. Do you know what's in it?"

"No," Bartley said indignantly. "I've never seen any such book myself."

"Well, I think Lillie might have a point. And now that I think about it, didn't it seem like he wanted us to head in this direction, like he was pushing to head this way with all that business about northern exposures and whatnot? If Lillie's

right and he really is taking us someplace, I want to know where."

"Then why don't you just ask him?" Bartley said. "Dr. Livingston is one of the world's great naturalists, a full professor at one of the world's finest universities! Just ask him."

I looked at Bartley for a long time, then back at Lillie. The light was failing, and the marsh was coming to life with the sounds of night insects. The first fireflies were already buzzing above the water like flickering candles, and the first deep-throated calls of bullfrogs were beginning to float up from the sawgrass. Somewhere out there, Tiger's mystery stalker might be watching us, and I expected Dr. Livingston to return at any minute from his lonely excursion. Somehow, I was sure he wouldn't return with any flowers. In fact, he hadn't collected a single flower since we'd been in Pa-Hay-Okee.

That gave me an idea.

"Okay," I said. "I'll ask him. But on one con-dition. If he doesn't give us a straight answer, then you agree to help us get a look at the book one way or the other, without him knowing, if need be."

Bartley huffed out an angry sigh. "Fine," he said. "But you'll see. There's nothing to this. Lillie," he said, turning to her, "you'll see."

Chapter Ten

The Map Book

Dr. Livingston returned to camp not long afterward, and sure enough, his pockets and hands were empty. He smiled as he strolled back through the woods, looking about at the trees.

He seemed the same as he always had: happy to be in the marsh and dignified, just like a professor should be. I wasn't so sure about our plan now, and for a minute, it seemed foolish to indulge Lillie's suspicions.

But then I reminded myself I had seen the book too, and our little trickery wasn't going to hurt anybody. If Bartley was right, as was likely, then nothing ventured, nothing gained.

"Well?" the professor asked Bartley as he sat near the fire ring, removing his jacket as he reclined. "Tell me. What did you find?"

Bartley stuttered for a few minutes, and personally, I thought he was just about the worst actor ever born. Even I could tell he was nervous, but Dr. Livingston just sat and listened to Bartley's account of flowers. Bartley was naming off all kinds of rare orchids, but Dr. Livingston hardly reacted at all.

Bartley had promised that Dr. Livingston would care about the flowers he was bragging about.

Strike one.

While Bartley talked, I helped Tiger with dinner. Once again, Tiger had done himself proud. Earlier that afternoon, he had used his knife to cut open the top of a cabbage palm and remove the ivory-colored heart, which he had wrapped in a piece of damp cloth. Now he was slicing the palm heart into thin strips and adding it to a pot full of crabs he had caught along the shore, plus a plug of salted, smoked pork for flavor. My mouth started watering.

When the stew was bubbling nicely, it was my turn to be the actor. I sat back on my rock and crossed my ankles. I was suddenly nervous, but I tried not to let it show. "So Dr. Livingston," I said in my best casual voice, interrupting Bartley. "I wonder if you think we're headed in the right direction."

"Well I sure do," he said, turning away from Bartley. "That is, if you do. As I've said, you're the guide here, Charlie."

"Yeah, I was wondering though, because, ah, well…" Then the next words got stuck in my throat. I wasn't accustomed to confronting adults, and it felt like I was accusing him of lying.

Luckily, Lillie came to the rescue. "What my brother's trying to say," she said, "is that if you got a map of where we're heading, it sure would be helpful. That is, if you got a map."

"A map?" Dr. Livingston said, and a flash of anger crossed his features for just a second before he looked like his normal self again. "Why no, Miss Lillie, I don't know that there are maps of this wilderness."

Strike two.

He had lied about the map.

"Right," I said, grateful that Lillie had done the heavy lifting but now hoping she would pipe down. "So I was thinking that maybe we should turn around because these islands here, well, they don't look like much."

Now I was sure of it. Dr. Livingston's eyes narrowed, and his face colored slightly. "Well no, Charlie," he said. "I suppose I don't think that's a very good idea. It strikes me that this is the right direction, based on my calculations." Then he took a deep breath, filling his chest up and sticking his chin out. I could just imagine him in front of a class of students with that same look on his face. "That is, unless you know how to locate the particular orchids that I'm looking for better than I."

Strike three.

He had refused to head back, even though I was supposed to be the guide.

It took everything I had not to look at Bartley, because it was plain as day that Dr. Livingston didn't seem to care at all about the rare orchids Bartley was finding, hadn't told the truth about the map, and now he didn't want to turn back even though he had said over and over I was the guide.

I was sure now that Lillie had been right. He was leading us somewhere.

"Um, Professor?" Bartley almost squeaked. "Sorry to interrupt, but that's just what I was telling you. I think Lillie and I, well—"

"We found a ghost orchid!" she interjected loudly and excitedly. "I'm sure of it! It was just like you said, Professor, nothing but roots on the side of the tree with these white flowers with big sepals, growing right on a clump of moss just like you predicted."

From the corner of my eye, I saw Tiger grinning with his head down over the steaming pot. Lillie was putting on a show that must have rivaled anything seen on Broadway in New York City.

Dr. Livingston just looked confused as his glance shifted from Bartley to Lillie and back again. "You don't say?" he said.

"No, it's true!" Lillie jumped up and tugged on Dr. Livingston's sleeve. "Come on! We'll show you!"

Bartley stood up too, so Dr. Livingston had little choice but to get up and follow them into the woods, looking for the imaginary orchid. As they headed into the trees, Lillie turned and winked at me, then pointed at Dr. Livingston's coat, which was still sitting on the rock where he left it.

"She good," Tiger said while I waited for them to disappear into the trees.

As soon as they were gone, I bolted to Dr. Livingston's coat and slid my hand inside the inner pocket. My fingers enclosed around a heavy brass instrument and a thin book. I yanked them out while Tiger left his stew to join me.

"Look!" I said. "I know what this is! It's a sextant."

The metal instrument was larger than I realized at first and more complicated. It had an eyepiece like a miniature telescope that looked through a little glass pane. Below that, there was a crescent-shaped brass bar with markings for degrees. Tiger took it from me and looked through the eyepiece, frowning slightly. He handed it back.

"So? What it do?" he said.

"It's a navigational tool," I said. "They use them on ships to find longitude and latitude." Tiger still looked confused, and I realized his education probably didn't include such subjects as chart navigation. "When ships are at sea, the captains don't know where they are, right? Because there's no land in sight. So they can use this device to figure out exactly where they are located by looking at the sun and stars. That way, they can make sure they never get lost."

"Huh," Tiger said.

"But why does Dr. Livingston have a sextant here? These aren't cheap, you know, and…" I let it trail off and opened up the book.

I could see right away that it was a very old book with brittle, yellow pages and a cracked leather cover. I turned the first page carefully and frowned. It was in Spanish, in a big cursive script that I couldn't read. I glanced at Tiger and he shrugged.

Then I flipped the next page and my eyes widened. I didn't need to know Spanish to understand the words written there:

"*Santiago*, Juan Ponce de León, Cuaderno de Bitacora, Anno Domini MDXIII"

I didn't know much about Ponce de León, except that he was the Spanish explorer who discovered Florida before even the Seminoles lived here. But that was just about it.

"What it say?" Tiger asked, leaning over the page.

"I'm not sure," I said. "I can't read it. You know who Ponce de León is?"

Tiger shook his head no.

"He was a Spanish explorer who discovered Florida for the Europeans. He supposedly named Florida after the Spanish word for the Feast of Flowers, because it was Easter time when he arrived here."

Tiger nodded. "Feast of Flowers? They ate flowers?"

"No, least I don't think so. It was just called that in Spain. The holiday."

I heard a noise in the woods and looked up quickly. Nobody was there. It must have been an animal.

But I knew I didn't have much time, so I started flipping through the stiff pages. It was all in Spanish, written in an ornate cursive script, and the letters were partly faded. It looked like a diary, but I couldn't even make sense out of the dates, except for MDXIII, which is the date 1513 in Roman numerals. I guess that was the year, but I wasn't sure.

Just when I was about to close the book halfway through, I came across a page with a map. Now this was more like it. Maps I could understand.

Tiger and I crowded close together and thumbed through page after page of maps, hoping to see something we recognized.

"Boy, I hope they didn't use these for navigation," I said. "If this is Florida, I sure don't recognize it."

"Me either," Tiger said.

I leafed through a few more maps until they ended suddenly and the pages went blank. I flipped back to the last map and studied it closely.

This last page showed a cluster of islands with a tiny, ornate cross smack in the middle of the cluster and something written in Spanish underneath it.

I looked up at Tiger.

"What?" he said. "What it mean?"

"I don't know, but…you think this could be a treasure map?"

He shrugged. "Could be."

I knew from personal experience that the Spanish spent a lot of time in the New World looking for gold. After all, I'd found a Spanish wreck loaded with gold doubloons a few years back, and Mama and Papa later used some of the gold to send Lillie to a fancy boarding school. Unfortunately, that gold was all gone now.

"You really think this could be a treasure map?" I said again, growing more excited. "No wonder Dr. Livingston is paying me $5 a day! He's looking for gold!"

Just then, we really did hear noises in the forest. Lillie was singing at the top of her lungs, I guess as a way to warn us they were coming back. Hurrying, I stuffed the book and the sextant back into Dr. Livingston's coat and huddled with Tiger around the stew just in time to see them coming out of the forest. Lillie and Bandit were leading the way, with Lillie marching and singing, and Bartley and Dr. Livingston looking miserable and bug-bitten as evening fell over our little camp.

Chapter Eleven

A Fight at Camp

Dr. Livingston sat down on a rock, mopped the sweat from his face, and shot Bartley a sour look. "Well, that was a lot of nothing," he said.

Bartley looked down. "Sorry, it must have been a trick of the light."

The professor snorted, then turned to look at the stewpot, dismissing Bartley. "So what's for dinner tonight, Tiger? I smell something interesting."

Nearby, I could feel Lillie trying to catch my eye, and Bartley just kept his head down.

"Charlie?" Lillie said. "Can you help me for a minute?"

She sauntered to the shoreline, down by the canoe, and was rooting around in our supplies like she was looking for something. I sighed. I knew I'd have to come clean with Lillie sooner or later, or she would just pester me until I did. I just hoped she could contain herself once she found out she had been right. But I could still try to postpone it as long as possible.

"What do you need, Lillie?" I called back, not moving from the fireside.

"Just come here for a spell, would you?" she said.

If Dr. Livingston thought anything was out of the ordinary, he didn't give a sign of his suspicions. Instead, he held out his dented tin bowl while Tiger spooned out a helping of his stew.

I got up and walked down to the shoreline, where Lillie was facing away from camp. I looked out over the darkening sawgrass, to the flicker of the ghostly fireflies and the small, dark bats flitting through the clouds of evening bugs. Again, I wondered if Tiger's mysterious watcher was out there, and if it was an animal or a human.

"So?" she whispered. "What'd you find?"

"You were right," I whispered back, but before she could respond, I went on, "but you can't say anything. We have to figure out how to handle this ourselves."

"Handle what?"

"He's not looking for flowers. He's got maps leading somewhere else—"

"I knew it!" she said triumphantly. "Didn't I tell you he was lying? I told you, didn't I?"

"Shhh!" I hissed. "Listen, Lillie, I'm still not completely sure—"

"Well what does the book say, Charlie?" she interrupted.

"That's the thing, I can't read it," I said.

"What do you mean you can't read it? Mama taught you how to read, didn't she?"

"I can't read it because it's in Spanish. So there's no reason to be rash yet, until we can figure out—"

"Spanish!" she said. "Oh my! I bet it's treasure! He's come here looking for treasure from another Spanish ship, just like the one you found!"

"That's what I thought too, but the maps are very old, Lillie. I think we should be careful how we—"

"He should tell us, Charlie," she interrupted again. "If he's got a treasure map, if he took us all this way to find something, he should tell us. You know he should. He should at least share it."

"Lillie," I said hopelessly, "I agree with you, but I think we should be careful how we—"

But she had already turned away and marched back up the beach toward the fire. It was dark enough now that the evening had closed like a fist around the firelight. We could only see their faces and the moths fluttering around the edges of the campfire.

"Professor?" Lillie said, barging back into the camp.

"Lillie!" I exclaimed, hurrying after her. "Wait!"

"Yes?" Dr. Livingston said, looking up from his soup.

Before I could get another word out, Lillie said, "Where are you taking us?"

Everything in camp went still for a second, and I swear even the mosquitoes and moths stopped for a heartbeat. Everybody stared at Lillie. Even Bartley looked up at her, astonished. Dr. Livingston looked confused. Tiger looked amused. And I tried my best to interrupt.

"I'm sorry?" Dr. Livingston said in his polite, dignified voice. "I'm not quite sure I catch your meaning."

"Lillie!" I said, catching up and taking ahold of her arm.

She shook me off and crossed her arms. "I mean with the maps and that device you're hiding. Where are you taking us?"

Dr. Livingston took in a deep breath, then let it out slowly. He set his bowl of stew down and stood up, and it made me realize how very tall and large he was. He was a full-grown man, at least a head taller than me. "I'm not sure I like the tone of your question," he said imperiously.

"Well?" Lillie said, standing her ground with her hands on her hips. "Where are you taking us?"

"I told you where. We're looking for flowers—"

"Uh uh," Lillie said. "You got secret maps in your book there. Old Spanish maps. Are you a treasure hunter?"

"A treasure hunter?" Dr. Livingston said. "Why, Miss Lillie, if I had known you were given to flights of fancy, I never would have agreed to let you come along."

"Flights of fancy!" she said. "It's right there in your jacket!" She pointed. "You know it is! You got a treasure map in there!"

"Miss Lillie," he said, switching to a soothing tone of voice, like he was talking to a fussy baby. "You should know better than to tell stories. I can understand having an active imagination, but honestly, a treasure map? Out here?" He swept his arm wide to include the buzzing marsh. "The only treasures out here are the biological kind."

Now Lillie might be as stubborn as a mule and hot-headed, but she was not a liar, and I wasn't going to stand by and watch while Dr. Livingston called my little sister a liar. I could tell it was hurting her feelings too, and underneath her angry expression, I saw the beginnings of frustrated tears welling up in her eyes.

"She's not lying," I said, standing up quickly.

"I saw it, Dr. Livingston. I saw your map book and that sextant in your jacket."

Dr. Livingston turned to me now, and Tiger stood up too. Bartley looked like he wanted to crawl into a hole and vanish. The mood in the camp grew tense.

"You looked through my private belongings?" Dr. Livingston said in a voice that was tight with controlled fury.

"It's like she said," I went on, trying to keep my voice steady and not let on that I was shaking like a leaf. "If you've got somewhere you really want to go, you should just tell me. You hired me to take you out here, but I can't do that unless I know where you really want to go."

Dr. Livingston looked at me in silence for a good, long spell, and I refused to look away first, even though I could feel my heart thumping in my chest like a wild hare on the run. Finally, he looked over at Tiger, then to Lillie, and lastly down at Bartley, who was still sitting on his rock looking unhappy.

"I see," he said, and suddenly the old familiar smile slipped back on his face. It took me by surprise. He went on, "Well, there's no reason for all this unpleasantness, is there? I see you've searched my things, and as angry as I have every right to be about that, I concede you have a point. You would be a more effective guide if I shared with you my goal. Now, however, there's too little light for me to show you everything I would need to show you. Why don't we revisit this first thing in the morning? How does that sound?"

"I suppose that sounds good," I said, sitting down slowly while Dr. Livingston also sank back onto his rock and resumed eating. "Tomorrow morning it is."

"Excellent," he said. "And Tiger," he raised his spoon at my friend, "once again, you've outdone yourself."

We finished the rest of the meal in uneasy silence. Then we threw some wet logs on the fire to smoke out the worst of the mosquitoes and lay down on the dry ground to sleep. I expected to have trouble sleeping, but after another hard day of slogging through the swamp and the emotional scene around the fire, I winked right out to sleep like a candle in a breeze. The last thing I heard was Tiger snoring next to me.

When I woke up the next morning, the first thing I heard was Lillie using a word that Mama would have punished her for even thinking. Then I heard Bartley moaning and Tiger saying something in Seminole. I sat up and shook the sleep from my eyes.

Bartley was sitting on the rock around the fire pit with the Wardian case between his knees.

Lillie was kicking at logs and punching the air.

And Tiger was down by the water, leaned over so far his nose was almost in the mud.

I didn't see Dr. Livingston right away.

"What's going on?" I said. "Where's the professor?"

Lillie turned and advanced on me like she was going to kick me. "He's gone, Charlie. And he took everything! All our food! Our canoe! Even the compass and your William Lauderdale rifle! Everything!"

Bartley groaned again.

"Tiger?" I said, climbing to my feet and letting my sleeping blanket fall to the ground. As Tiger looked up, I realized with a sinking feeling that the canoe wasn't bobbing in the water with its stacks of food and supplies and my prized rifle.

"He gone," Tiger said. "We in trouble. Big trouble."

Chapter Twelve

Betrayed

"Bartley," I said, "what's going on?"

He looked up from his Wardian case, distraught. "I don't know, Charlie," he said. "I was hoping you could tell me. What was in that book?"

I wasn't sure how to answer. After all, Bartley was his assistant, and it only made sense that Bartley knew more than he was letting on.

Then again, Dr. Livingston had abandoned Bartley too, so I figured I could trust him.

"I don't know," I said. "The book was in Spanish, so I couldn't read any of it. There were a bunch of old maps and the name Ponce de León on the front page."

"Ponce de León?" Bartley said. "The conquistador?"

"I guess," I said. "Why? Does that mean something to you?"

Bartley thought for a second. "Well, no, I can't say that it does."

"Do you know anything about him?"

Bartley sighed. "I'm a naturalist, Charlie. We don't take a lot of history classes. I know de León was the governor of Puerto Rico when he sailed west to discover Florida. If I remember correctly, he had a run-in here with a particularly fierce band of Indians, the Calusa I think they were called. They eventually ended up killing him with an arrow."

"What about gold?" I said. "You think he was looking for gold?"

"Well of course he was looking for gold," Bartley said. "Or something of value. All the Spanish in those days were looking for gold."

"Huh."

Bartley frowned at me. "Wait a second. Is that what you're thinking? That this a gold hunt?"

"I don't reckon I know," I said, "but that sure did look like a treasure map, and you just said yourself all the Spanish were after gold."

Bartley shook his head at me. "No, that's not possible. Dr. Livingston's already a wealthy man, Charlie. He lives in very comfortable circumstances. He doesn't care about gold."

"All men care about gold," I said, "especially when there's lots of it. And if it's not gold, then you tell me. Why else would he leave us out here stranded for dead?"

Bartley fell silent again and stared moodily at

the ground. I turned away from him, toward Tiger. "What do we still got?"

While Bartley and I had been talking, Tiger had piled all of our remaining items together. It was a pitifully small pile: Tiger's short knife, our four sleeping blankets, and the stewpot. Plus Bartley's Wardian case full of orchids.

My rifle was gone, along with just about everything else. Fishing line and hooks. Tiger's cast net and harpoon. The compass. Salt. The flint and steel. Spare clothes and shoes. The mosquito nets. Water containers. And all food whatsoever.

I was already growing hungry for breakfast.

"What're we gonna do, Charlie?" Lillie asked.

I swallowed hard. Up until this point, I didn't think I'd been a very good guide. Mostly, I felt like I'd led us wandering around the sawgrass for days on end with precious little direction. But now was the time for leadership. Now there were decisions to be made, and no one said it out loud, but we all knew the truth: we could die out here.

I started talking slowly, thinking while I was talking. "As far as I see it, we got two choices. We can go back, or we can go after our things. Going back means days or even weeks of hard travel with no supplies and no food. Going forward means pushing further into the swamp and trying to find Dr. Livingston somewhere out there." I looked up and over the sawgrass, where the breaking morning sun glinted off open water and made the grass shine green. "Neither is great, but personally, I'm for going after him. He can't be too far ahead of us, and I don't reckon he'll be able to go much faster than us either. He's not from these parts, and Pa-Hay-Okee doesn't give up its secrets easily. I think it shouldn't be too hard to track him down."

Tiger nodded along and Bartley didn't object, which was good enough for me.

"What about breakfast?" Lillie asked hopefully.

I looked helplessly at her. "Sorry, Lil. We're just gonna have to tighten our belts for now. We'll do what we can."

Before we left the island, we scoured it for anything we could use. Tiger found a strong, straight piece of black ironwood that he quickly carved into a spear. Meanwhile, Lillie and I took the stewpot down to the water and collected as many crabs and mussels as we could, then put them into the pot, where the crabs skittered around.

When we were finally ready to set out, Bartley refused to leave behind his little glass house full of flowers, until I told him if he wanted to bring it, he'd have to carry it himself. So he left it in a protected spot and looked as sad as I'd ever seen a grown man look when we finally waded away.

I led us in the general direction I'd seen Dr. Livingston looking the night before, but it was impossible to tell if he'd come this way. Even for a Seminole, it was impossible to track someone through Pa-Hay-Okee. The soft bottom of muck and marl didn't hold any footprints, and the sawgrass and reeds held no record of anyone passing.

I had little to go on except hope and a stewpot full of skittering crabs wrapped in a blanket and bumping against my back.

It was slow going all day. Tiger was careful to inspect every blade of grass for signs of Dr. Livingston, while we made every effort to collect food. Just before midday, Tiger called for us to hush, then moved as fast as a rattlesnake and speared a turtle. I hadn't even seen it swimming by, and he grinned when he held up his homemade spear with lunch on its end.

"Good job," I said.

We lunched on a narrow spit of land with a hard shelf of blinding white coral rocks and a few scraggly trees. Even though we didn't have a flint, Tiger dug a small trench the size of his hand, then laid a thick palm frond stem over it. He next found a small stick that he sharpened into a point. Spinning the stick between his hands, he rubbed the point into the palm frond. He gave Lillie a handful of the dried moss and told her to be ready for a spark. After a few minutes of working and spinning the little stick, a puff of smoke rose up.

"Now!" Tiger said, and Lillie shoved a little bit of the moss under the smoking stick. A tiny red ember was born in the moss, then Tiger took the

clump of moss into his hands. Very carefully, like he was handling a baby bird, he blew on it until the ember flickered into a flame and we had a fire.

"Well done, Tiger!" I exclaimed. "On your first try!"

Tiger beamed with pride, and even though we had nothing but a few soggy blankets and an old dented stewpot, we ate a fairly satisfying lunch of boiled turtle, crabs and mussels. It could have used a pinch or two of salt, but I wasn't about to complain.

After lunch, we went on, noticing that the water was growing more shallow and the sawgrass was giving way to tender green reeds that rose only a foot or so out of the water. Heat rose in waves off the water, and I began to worry that we had made a mistake in coming this direction. There was no sign of Dr. Livingston.

But I didn't let fear take hold, and when Bartley started to worry that we might not make it home, I told him he needed to keep those kinds of thoughts to himself.

"Listen," I said, "we're going to be just fine. Tiger here can catch anything we need and cook it up. And my little sister here once walked nearly the entire length of Florida by herself with nothing but a little sack of grits. It's Dr. Livingston who should be worried about us catching up to him."

Bartley fell silent, and we kept on.

In the hottest part of the afternoon, when the sun poured down unrelenting heat, we came across a wide channel cutting through the shallow marsh. The water in the channel was murky with sediment and ran faster than the shin-deep, clear water where we stood. The banks of the channel were marked with tufts of cattails.

"I don't think we should cross here," Lillie said, eyeing the water. "We don't know how deep that is. Could be anything in there."

"Anything? What's that mean?" Bartley asked.

"*Allapattah,*" Tiger muttered. "On the bottom. Or in grass."

"*Allapattah?*" Bartley repeated.

"Alligator," I said.

Just then, a dark snout and a pair of eyes popped to the surface on the far side of the channel. Two more rose next to it, and we saw their long, dark bodies shadowed just under the surface.

Bartley took a step backward and almost fell over.

I glanced at him. "Don't worry," I said. "Long as we leave them alone, they'll leave us alone. But Lillie's right. No way we can cross here."

We began walking alongside the wide channel, hoping for a shallow place where we could cross without running into a hoard of hungry alligators. The far bank was crawling with the big reptiles. Fortunately, there were none on our side, and we made sure to watch the bottom carefully. You sure don't want to step on a gator.

At one point, we saw a small piece of dry land on the far bank. It wasn't longer than six feet and was crowned with grasses and cattails. Three of the big reptiles had pulled themselves up onto the dry land to bake in the sun, and we stopped to study them. There was something different about these gators. They were lighter in color, instead of the dark, almost black color I was used to. And their legs were shorter and snouts were pointier.

"Hey Lillie," I said. "You notice anything strange about those gators?"

She looked for a minute, then she said, "Hey! Those aren't gators, Charlie! They're crocodiles! Look at their teeth!"

"That's what I thought," I said. Florida crocodiles were rare, but you could always tell one by its teeth. Crocodiles' teeth show when their mouths are closed, whereas alligator teeth are hidden when their mouths are closed. I was glad they were on the other side. Crocs are a lot more dangerous and aggressive than alligators.

We went on without disturbing the big crocs, and before long, we stopped seeing them altogether. By this time, the channel had narrowed and the current seemed stronger. Small islands and land had begun to appear on the far side of the channel, looking like a maze

of hammocks intercut with stretches of open water, sawgrass, and more channels. I couldn't be sure, but the sight of it raised my hopes. It looked like the clusters of islands I'd seen on Dr. Livingston's map, and I kept my eyes sharp for any sign of him.

When we hadn't seen a croc in a long time, we crossed the channel, swimming across quickly and making enough noise and commotion to scare away anything hiding in the nearby grass. We climbed out of the shallow water on the other side, then began walking again. We'd only gone a short ways when Tiger called out, "Charlie! Come! Look!"

Tiger was looking at something on the water. I hurried over, followed by Lillie, Bandit, and Bart-ley. At first, I couldn't tell what he was looking at. There was another little channel cutting through the muck to join the bigger one we had been walking along.

"What?" I said.

Slowly, carefully, Tiger reached out and grabbed a piece of wood bobbing on the surface. He lifted it, and I went in for a closer look. It came up with a green cord attached to it, like a float. Looking closely, my forehead almost touching Tiger's, I saw where a groove had been cut into the wood and a braided cord made from green plant fiber was looped around it. The cord trailed away into the water.

"Strange," I said. "What do you think it is?"

Tiger grabbed the cord and pulled on it. It didn't budge at first, then all of a sudden, there was a splashing sound and I saw four more of the wood floats go under. They were strung in a row across the narrow channel. I helped him pull, and before long, we had dislodged a net made from that same plant fiber. It had been strung across the place where the smaller channel joined the larger channel. I held the float on one end while Tiger held the float on the other end, and Lillie and Bartley helped us lift the net up so we could all see it. The strands were slimy with green algae.

The fine net was made from swamp reeds that had been rolled and braided into strong ropes, then woven into a perfect net. It was attached on the top to the four wood bobbers Tiger had discovered, and on the bottom, the net was securely fastened to two large conch shells.

"Conch don't live anywhere near here," I said. "Those shells were brought here from the ocean."

"Thanks, Charlie," Lillie said sarcastically. "I think we figured that out by now."

"Fish gate," Tiger said. "It's a fish gate."

I saw what he meant. By blocking off the smaller channel, somebody—or maybe more than one somebody—was preventing fish from swimming out of this area.

But who?

I looked up the dark line of the smaller channel, following it to where it disappeared in the cluster of islands. Once again, my mind crowded with visions of desperate fugitives hiding in the swamps, but then whoever had made this knew how to live in the swamp.

I had a feeling they were somewhere nearby, probably on one of the small islands. I had a feeling Dr. Livingston was in those islands too, and I remembered his map with the cross right in the center.

"C'mon," I said. "We should follow this channel up into yonder islands. But keep an eye out. I have a feeling we're hot on Livingston's trail."

Chapter Thirteen

The Indian in the Woods

We began passing small bits of land, then larger islands. They were covered with trees and vines, with bright slashes of shining white where coral rock lay exposed to the sun like bone.

The channel ran straight and true, cutting between small islands like an arrow.

"Tiger," I said, "what do you think this is? I think this was dug here on purpose."

He nodded. "I thinking same thing. Too straight."

"Who would dig such a thing?" Bartley asked. "And more importantly, how?"

"Don't know," I said.

Soon we began passing smaller channels, sometimes with more of the wood floats strung across them, and these too were perfectly straight.

I figured there were nets in these also, making this place a sort of fish farm.

"Look!" Tiger said, pointing up into a tree.

A cormorant bird was fluttering up from a branch, but it couldn't fly away and was squawking loudly. A thin cord ran from the bird's leg to a green sapling that had been tied to the larger branch. It was a snare. And whoever set it hadn't come this way to collect their catch yet. Someone was close by.

"Here now, Charlie," Bartley said, "I think we should turn back. This obviously isn't the work of Professor Livingston. It feels like we're trespassing on Indian land, and I for one have no desire to be scalped."

I glanced back at Tiger, hoping that Bartley hadn't insulted him. Tiger and his people were sensitive to the fear that many white people had about Indians. Fortunately, Tiger didn't look like he was paying much attention.

"We're not going to be scalped," I said. "Besides, if someone does live here, they might be able to help us. We'll need to eat sometime today. Anyway, I have a feeling Dr. Livingston is headed in this same direction."

"That's right," he said sarcastically. "Your treasure map."

"Shh," I said. "Let's not be any louder than we have to."

We walked on, passing small hammocks that were alive with the sound of birds and buzzing insects, and every so often the water sloshed with the sound of a turtle or fish rolling on the surface.

Soon we came to a place where the channel curved around a flat, dense hammock. We followed it around to where it emptied into a sort of hidden pool. The pool was ringed with small islands that had narrow channels cutting between them. A fish pierced the surface of the water, and I saw that the pool was ringed with floats, so whatever swam in here wouldn't be able to get out. Another fish rolled on the surface, and I guessed that the whole pool was thick was fish.

A slight breeze blew through the trees, and I jumped at the sound. The trees came alive with the clanking of amulets and carvings that had been suspended from the branches. There must have been a hundred of the carvings, all ringing in the wind like chimes. There were masks and birds and fish carved into wood, shells, and pieces of bone.

But the biggest surprise by far lay on a larger island across the small pool. A clearing had been cut from the tall hardwoods, and a small mound rose between the trees. A small, strangely shaped hut sat atop the mound. It was made from woven palm fronds, like a Seminole chickee hut, but its shape was different. The roof was flared like a bell with a chimney hole in the middle, and the walls were solid. A small garden with wild herbs, root vegetables, and coontie grew next to the mysterious little house.

"Tiger," I whispered, "what is this place?"

He shook his head. "Don't know."

"You think anybody's home?" Lillie asked.

"I don't know," I said.

"I think we should leave," Bartley said.

I wasn't sure what to do next, but I didn't feel any danger here. With the sun slanting through the surrounding trees onto the shallow pool with its fish corral, and the chimes sounding in the trees, the feeling of this place was peaceful. I felt the need to be respectful of this place.

"I think we'll be all right to get closer," I said. "But we should stay together."

We began walking around the edge of the pond, sticking close to the shore. But we had no sooner made it halfway around when Bartley stumbled on a sunken log and splashed loudly.

"Bartley!" I said.

But he never had a chance to answer before we were all silenced by a sharp call from the trees to our side. Tiger whirled around, peering into the trees of the hammock and raising his spear. Lillie uttered a short cry.

"Wait!" I said. "Tiger, no!"

We stopped and waited until a figure emerged from the dark trees, moving as silently as a heron gliding over the water and seeming to vanish and flicker into the background as he approached. Slowly he came into full view, and Lillie caught her breath.

The Indian's entire body was painted with stripes and whorls of black ink, and his face was dyed red with black streaks across his forehead and cheeks. The only hint I had of his age was his white hair, which was tied into a topknot on his head. He wore only the skimpiest of cloths around his waist, but he had a band of colored shells tied around his throat, and both wrists were similarly decorated with large bracelets made from colorful shells. Both ears were pierced with curved bones. He was very thin, but he looked strong and his eyes were clear and black.

In one hand he held a club with a sharp, jagged edge. I saw that he had decorated the club with shark's teeth, and I shivered at the thought of the damage it could do.

"Tiger," I said, trying to keep my voice calm. "Put your spear down."

The Indian kept his eyes on Tiger, never looking away until Tiger slowly lowered his spear. He didn't speak.

"What now?" Lillie said.

"Be friendly," I muttered back. "Let's not give him any reason to use that club."

In a louder voice, I called out, "Hello? Sir?"

The Indian looked my way and his eyes narrowed, but he didn't speak.

"Sir? Do you speak English?"

When he didn't answer, Tiger said, *"Istonko?"* but didn't receive an answer. From the Indian's expression, it was impossible for me to figure out if

he meant us harm. I felt like he was making some kind of decision, but I couldn't guess what it was.

He took a step closer to us, and it was everything I could do not to step back or crowd in front of my sister.

"Charlie," Lillie said. "What should we do?"

Then two things happened. First, Bandit, who had been exploring alongside us all day, showed up and scampered around Lillie's feet. The Indian looked at the raccoon, then up at my sister. His cheeks wrinkled in a sudden smile.

Second, Bartley began to talk, and the Indian's head swiveled toward him. I couldn't understand a word Bartley was saying because he was talking in Spanish, but when he was done, the Indian nodded and held up one hand. He uttered something back in a deep voice, and I recognized it as Spanish.

Bartley nodded and replied.

"How'd you know he spoke Spanish?" I asked.

He shrugged. "I had a hunch."

Then the Indian said something else to Bartley and turned his back on us. He began to glide through the woods, heading toward the hut.

"Where's he going?" I asked.

"I think home," Bartley said. "He wants us to follow him."

Chapter Fourteen

A Strange Tea Party

We followed the Indian along a narrow trail. The chimes sounded overhead, and I saw where he had carved the living bark of trees into the shape of turtles and fish and even people. The Indian moved along the path without making a sound, like he was gliding through the trees. When he reached the end of the little island, he lightly jumped across the channel and continued on around toward his house. We all jumped after him.

The small hut was a solid structure with thick posts that had been sunk deep into the mound.

The thatchwork was as good as any I'd ever seen in a Seminole village, and he had mounted a buck's skull complete with antlers over the small door. He stopped under the skull and faced us, then said something else in Spanish and went inside.

"What'd he say?" I asked Bartley.

"He invited us in," Bartley said, looking at the dark door with something like terror on his face. "But I don't think we follow him in there. I'm not sure this is a good idea—"

"We're being rude," Lillie said. "Of course we should go in."

I was first in, followed by the others, and lastly by Bandit. The floor of the hut was hard-packed dirt, and it took a minute for my eyes to adjust to the gloom. A large animal skin lay on the ground near one wall, and I thought it looked like a panther. I had to duck to avoid the many implements and containers hanging from the rafters. There were cups and bowls made from gourds, as well as various other tools made from shells and bone. A fire ring made from coral rock was in the middle of the hut, with a little tepee of kindling and twigs waiting to be lit.

My eyes settled on a large and toothy crocodile skull leaning against the back wall. The skull had been decorated with black and red paint just like the Indian's face, and it seemed to stare at us from its empty eye sockets.

The Indian faced us, put a hand on his chest, and began talking in Spanish to Bartley, who translated. "My name is Pah-pat-ukale, the last of the Calusa warriors," he said. "I have been expecting you many of these long years."

I looked at Bartley, wondering if he'd translated it wrong. Expecting us? A Calusa? I remembered Bartley saying something about Ponce de León and the Calusa, but I'd never heard of them before. The only Indians I knew were Seminole.

I looked more closely at him. It was hard to tell how old he was exactly, with all the pigments and adornments on his body, but he looked like

the most ancient person I'd ever seen. And yet…
he didn't look like other old people I had seen
in the past. They were stooped over and often
walked with canes or crutches. But not the Calusa. He stood straight and strong. His body was
wiry with muscles, and his eyes were clear.

"Bartley," Tiger said. "Translate for me."

Bartley translated as Tiger spoke: "Greetings. I
am Tiger Bowlegs of the Seminole people. Thank
you for your hospitality."

To me, Tiger said, "Now you, Charlie. Greet
him."

I snapped out of my shock. I had forgotten my
manners. While Bartley translated, I introduced
myself as Charlie Pierce, then Lillie introduced herself, and finally Bartley introduced himself as Jonathan Bartley from Yale. The Indian stared at each
of us as we talked. When we were done, he nodded
at Bandit, who was busy sniffing around some of
the bones and things on the ground.

"Who is this?" he said.

"That's Bandit," Lillie answered proudly. "He's
my friend."

"Raccoons do make good friends," he said.
"Now sit please. I will make tea."

Tea? I thought, watching in wonder as the old
Indian squatted before the fire pit. From a smaller
hole inside the pit, he carefully removed a bright

ember with two sticks and held it to the little pile of tinder. Before long, a small fire was burning. He didn't seem to be in a hurry, and he didn't talk to us while he worked.

I leaned over to Bartley. "Bartley," I whispered. "What's this about the Calusa? You know anything about them?"

He shrugged. "I thought they'd been extinct for a hundred years."

"Don't tell him that."

Still ignoring us, the Calusa put a small bowl over the flames and poured water into it, then watched it patiently until steam rose and it started to boil. Then he mixed in a handful of dried leaves he retrieved from another nearby bowl. The air filled with a familiar smell, and I recognized the plant. We called it yaupon holly, but I'd never seen anyone make tea out of it.

After it had boiled for a few minutes, the Calusa carefully poured the hot tea into another gourd through a hole in its side. This gourd had a long neck like a spout. He surprised me by shaking the gourd until the tea inside was frothy. Finally, he got a highly polished conch shell hanging from the rafters and carefully poured a bit of the steaming tea into the shell. He looked around the circle at each of us in turn, then he poured a little of the tea onto the ground between us and took a sip.

"Hmm," he said through the steam. "It has been a long time since I made tea for visitors."

When he was done, he passed the gourd to Bartley, who also took a sip, then handed it to me. The tea was bitter and strong. I felt it warming me all the way down to my stomach.

I handed the conch to Lillie, who also took a sip and smiled. Just like the Indian, she said, "Hmmm."

After the conch had made the rounds, it went back to Pah-pat-ukale, who poured the rest on the ground between us, then looked up at us, again seeming to weigh us carefully.

"Um," I said after a minute or so of silence. "Sir, what did you mean you were expecting us?"

The tea seemed to sharpen my ears as Pah-pat-ukale sat with his eyes closed for a long minute, then began to speak.

"For many years, I have watched the white man and the Creek come closer and closer. My heart told me that, one day, there would be no place the white man would not find. But I had expected soldiers, not children and raccoons. I am not sorry to be wrong."

"Creek?" Tiger said. "My people come from the Creek."

Pah-pat-ukale turned his gaze on Tiger. "Yes, I recognize your features. Our people have fought, but we will not let that come between us today for you are very young and I am very old."

Tiger looked like he didn't know what to say.

"Um, Mr. Ukale," Lillie cut in before I could say anything else, "how come you can speak Spanish? I never met an Indian before that could speak Spanish."

Pah-pat-ukale smiled at Lillie. His teeth were white and large, and it figured that Lillie had already managed to make friends with him. I had the feeling that our reception might not have been as kind if Lillie and Bandit weren't with us.

"Ah, the questions of curious little girls," he said. "You have no idea how I've missed that."

"Well," Lillie said, "who taught you?"

"The man who taught me this language is long dead."

"Was he Spanish?" Lillie asked.

"Yes," Pah-pat-ukale said. "Like all the others, he too came here looking for Calusa treasure. But the Spanish think only of gold."

Treasure! I knew it! My ears perked up and I saw Bartley frown.

"But if he's dead, then who do you live with?" Lillie asked, looking around the little hut. "You don't live out here all by yourself, do you? That would be awful!"

"Not really alone," he said. "The Spanish may be gone but my people are still here."

Bartley stared in surprise while Pah-pat-ukale

explained: "In the old days, my people lived by the great water, where we fished and made our homes on the many islands. Our cacique ruled these swamps from our great village, where we had built a hut large enough to hold hundreds of our people. We collected tribute from all the tribes of the swamp. We were first among all the peoples. When the white man came, he asked us to submit. To believe in his god. But we would not bend to white man's will.

"My people believe that each of us has three souls. There is the first soul, which lives in your shadow. There is the second soul, which lives in your reflection in the calm waters. And there is the third soul, which lives in this part of your eye." He pointed to the black pupil in his eye. "When my people's bodies died, their shadow and water souls went to live in the animals of the swamp. But the eye soul, that soul stays with them forever."

"So you mean they're dead but their spirits are still here?" Lillie asked, looking a little nervous, like a troop of Indians might pop out at any minute.

"Yes. I buried the last of my warrior brothers here on this island. Their spirits keep me company when the loneliness becomes too much."

"Your warriors?" Tiger asked. "Are you a chief?"

Pah-pat-ukale shook his head when Bartley was done translating.

"No," he said. "I am not the cacique. He left with the rest of my people."

"Oh," Lillie said sadly. "You're alone."

I could tell she was feeling sorry for the old Indian, but I was thinking something else entirely. He had said it himself: he had stayed behind to protect the Calusa treasure. What's more, he spoke Spanish, and Dr. Livingston's book was in Spanish. It seemed obvious that he was here protecting the very same treasure Dr. Livingston was looking for. For all I knew, he had already found Dr. Livingston and taken care of him with his sharks' tooth club. The thought sent a chill down my arms, and I resolved to be careful with this Indian. Just because he served us tea didn't mean he was our friend.

"Excuse me," I said, with Bartley translating. "You said the Spanish came for the Calusa treasure? Did they, ah, ever find it?"

Pah-pat-ukale smiled a hard smile and his eyes flashed. For one second, I saw the fierce warrior he must have been in his younger days. "No," he said. "Nor has any other intruder. The Calusa were never defeated. Our treasure is still ours."

Again Bartley frowned, so I leaned over and said, "What's the matter? I told you Dr. Livingston had a treasure map!"

"It's not that," Bartley said. "It's that…I'm not sure how to translate what he's saying exactly. He keeps using a word I don't really recognize, and I think it's treasure, but…I'm not really sure. It sounds different."

I shrugged. "Maybe you're just not hearing him right."

"I'm telling you—" Bartley started.

The Calusa interrupted us, and Bartley turned to translate what he said.

"Now I have a question for you," Pah-pat-ukale said.

"Yes?" I answered.

"Why did your leader leave you in the swamp to die?"

"How do you know about that?" I asked.

"I've been watching you."

"Oh. Well, we're not exactly sure why," I said. "I think he left us because he's also looking for the Calusa treasure, but we didn't know until it was too late. He lied to us. He tricked us."

Pah-pat-ukale shook his head, and his eyes hardened with anger. "Once again, greed rules the hearts of white men." He stood up suddenly, quickly for a very old man. "Now," he said, "it is time to go find your deceiver."

Chapter Fifteen

Poisoned Arrows

Pah-pat-ukale reached over his head and untied a small gourd with a narrow opening and a crude wooden cork. He squatted and carefully removed the cork, then tipped out a tiny drop of sluggish sap into an oyster shell. He spat into the shell and mixed its contents with a small stick, then set it down and retrieved a small quiver with arrows in it. As he rolled the arrowheads in the mixture, I heard Bartley gasp.

"I know what that is!" he said. "That's manchineel sap! It's a poison!" He switched to Spanish and asked Pah-pat-ukale something, then translated. "I asked him if he means to kill Dr. Livingston."

"No!" Lillie said. "Of course he's not going to do that."

"You don't know that, Lillie," I said.

"Yes, I do!"

"No," Pah-pat-ukale said as Bartley translated. "This will not kill him. He will sleep as if dead, but he will wake."

When he finished, Pah-pat-ukale stood up and left his little hut quickly, leaving the rest of us to exchange grim looks.

"Now listen," Bartley said, "we can't just stand by and let that Indian kill Dr. Livingston—"

"Livingston left us to die," Tiger interrupted. "Why show him respect he does not show us?"

"This is ridiculous!" Bartley exclaimed. "Professor Livingston is one of the most respected naturalists in the world—"

"But I saw that map book myself—" I said.

"I told you!" Bartley almost shouted. "Professor Livingston doesn't care about Spanish gold! He's already a rich man! You were the one who told that Indian that the professor is looking for this treasure! Charlie Pierce, if he hurts Professor Livingston, I will hold you responsible for the crime!"

Tiger started to say something angry, and Lillie looked like she was spitting mad. I was angry too, but I had to calm things down.

"Bartley," I said, cutting off my friend and sister, "let's look at the facts. Dr. Livingston left us alone in the swamp. Even you must admit he didn't come out here to collect flowers. Did you see him take a single plant the whole way here?"

Bartley didn't answer.

"I'm sorry, Bartley," I said. "I really am. But

what's done is done. Treasure or no, we have to see this through to the end. It's either that or leave it up to Pah-pat-ukale!"

Bartley still looked angry, but he agreed. We hurried out of the hut to follow Pah-pat-ukale past his little vegetable garden and toward the back of the island. We jogged down a narrow path between the trees and finally caught up with him near the water's edge. There were three canoes on the shore. Two were turned upside down and didn't look like they'd been used in a long time. The third was decorated with bone and shell trinkets, and a pair of buck antlers was mounted on the bow.

Pah-pat-ukale glanced back at us, his expression unreadable. I was afraid Bartley would start shouting again, but he didn't. Instead, Pah-pat-ukale hesitated for a moment, then waved Tiger and Lillie into his canoe and shoved it offshore.

I quickly flipped over a second canoe for Bartley and me, then grabbed a long branch for a paddle. We pushed off the shore and followed the others down a wide canal between small islands. I was surprised to see that Pah-pat-ukale didn't paddle his canoe, but stood up on a platform in the back and poled it through the shallow water, somehow without making a sound. I tried to do the same, using my branch as a pole, but I almost fell into the water. I ended up on my knees, pushing frantically to keep up.

We went deeper and deeper into the thicket of islands. Everywhere there was the sound of insects, running water like a multitude of shallow

streams tumbling over rocks, and birds calling noisily from the trees. This area was different from any other place I had been in the great swamp of Pa-Hay-Okee. Here it felt like we were pushing deeper and deeper into a bright green jungle, and even the harsh sunlight seemed different, greener somehow.

"You really think Professor Livingston came this way?" Bartley asked, sounding like he didn't think so at all.

I was panting from trying to keep up with Pah-pat-ukale and the others. I had no idea how his canoe seemed to glide over the water like a bird through air while I felt like I was pushing us upstream against a heavy wind. "I don't know, Bartley," I said.

He fell into a moody silence, watching the shore go by on either side. Then he gave a slight gasp. "Look!" he said, pointing at the bank.

I stopped paddling for a second and stared at the shore. In the mud near the water was a set of wet footprints, like someone had struggled along this shore.

"Good eyes," I said to Bartley. "We might make a tracker out of you yet."

"You need good eyes to spot flowers on three continents," he said, still sounding annoyed but also a little proud.

I didn't say anything else as I worked on the branch pole like a maniac. Up ahead, the waterway split into two, and Pah-pat-ukale's canoe was already sliding silently out of sight. I'd lose him if I didn't pole faster.

Finally, we rounded the corner and headed into a narrower canal, this one like a tunnel of thick trees, their branches locking together overhead into an arch. It was dimmer here, and only occasional shafts of golden light pierced the thicket of branches and fell onto the water. Up ahead in the other canoe, Lillie turned around to look at us, and even from this far away, I could see her eyes were as wide as saucers.

Then I saw why.

There couldn't have been any other waterway on earth like this one. The trees alongside the banks were familiar — gumbo-limbo, bay, mahogany, even palms — but they were the largest I'd ever seen, with trunks as large as wagon wheels, and their twisted, ancient branches thicker than a full-grown man. Spanish moss as long as my body hung from their branches, which were festooned with hundreds of plants. Closer to the ground, leaves the size of barrel hoops nodded over the water. I stopped poling to gaze in shock at an orange and purple grasshopper the size of Papa's hand that was jumping from leaf to leaf before it vanished into the forest.

Bartley muttered in awe and gripped the sides of the canoe.

"You ever seen anything like this on three continents?" I asked him.

He shook his head. "No, can't say that I have."

"Me neither."

Up ahead, Pah-pat-ukale had stopped poling forward and his canoe was gliding along the narrow, twisting river, pulled as if by a light current. He looked back at me and held his hand out for me to stop paddling. I gratefully put my pole down and felt a slight current grab our canoe and pull us forward, beneath the magnificent canopy of vegetation.

Overhead, creepers and vines hung down from the trees, reaching for us like hairy and thick fingers. Before long, the thick vines were close enough overhead that I could almost grab them.

And that's exactly what Pah-pat-ukale did.

Silently, without warning, he reached up and grabbed a thick vine, then turned for me and motioned for me to do the same. I got up on the canoe platform, praying I wouldn't fall headlong into the water as the boat rocked beneath me. I swiped at passing vines until I finally got ahold of one. The gentle current tugged at us and almost pulled me over.

I was about to complain about hanging on these vines like a monkey when I heard Lillie say, "Oh my! Look, Tiger! Look!"

On the left bank, there rose a short wall of white coral rock that glistened with copper colored veins and pink hues like a conch shell. Trees grew up and over the rock, their roots lacing over its face like long tentacles gripping it firmly to the shore. Midway down the rock, there was a perfect hole, and a natural spout had formed to allow a little stream of clear water to gush into the canal. I had seen freshwater springs before, especially in the center of the state when I traveled with Papa. But I had never seen a spring come from the middle of a rock. I had the feeling that if I touched the water, it would be shockingly cold.

Pah-pat-ukale was staring at the stream too, his lips moving as if in a silent prayer.

"Hey!" I called to him, my voice too loud for the hushed waterway. "Why are we stopped here?"

Just then there was a muffled shout from the island, somewhere deep in the thick trees beyond the spring.

"What was that?" I said.

"Professor Livingston!" Bartley cried.

Pah-pat-ukale shouted something in his native tongue, then pushed his canoe toward the shore. He leaped from the canoe and landed on the shore, then plunged into the dense foliage and disappeared.

"Charlie!" Lillie called, looking back at me and holding onto a bush to keep the canoe from drifting away. "What do we do now?"

"Hold on!" I shouted. "We're coming!"

With a few shoves, we were at the rock too. All of us, including Bartley, climbed up the steep bank of sharp rocks and found ourselves on a ledge crowded with huge plants, facing a curtain of Spanish moss hanging from the giant trees. A narrow trail headed through the moss, and the sound of the hidden stream gurgled from deep within the trees.

I glanced at Tiger and Lillie. They were watching me, I guess for a sign of what we should do. Bartley was just staring at the moss.

"Charlie—?" Lillie started.

"C'mon," I said. "We've got to go after them."

Chapter Sixteen

Banyan Island

I jumped back as a butterfly the size of a dinner plate fluttered up from a huge flower nearby. I waved it away and kept running. The path ran alongside a narrow streambed that had cut its way through shining white coral rock. The fast-moving water gurgled happily, almost completely hidden by plants growing over the stream.

Behind me, Tiger, Lillie, Bandit, and Bartley ran to keep up.

I heard nothing from ahead because the leaves here were so dense that they cut off all the sound.

I was running into the bush, not sure what I'd find ahead, when I burst through a wall of vegetation and skidded to a stop. We were in a clearing at the top of the island. The place was ringed with a nearly perfect circle of banyan trees, their fluted trunks gripping the ground in a thousand places and their thick grey roots running over the exposed rock like coiled serpents. Through the far side of the clearing, a sharp bank dropped away, and I could see the bright marsh beyond.

Despite the great summer heat, this place was cool, with giant banyan leaves fluttering and falling noiselessly to the ground, adding to the thick carpet of dead leaves. Speckled sunlight fell through the branches above, lighting the scene below. The trees' branches were festooned with thousands of plants, many with flowers hanging down like long veils.

In the center of the clearing was a depression in the white coral rock. Pillows of green ferns grew around this natural basin and formed a kind of carpet. The stream issued from a narrow slit at the bottom of the basin, its clear water bubbling and boiling before rushing down the streambed toward the shoreline. A small tree grew near the basin, but it looked only half-alive, with most of its branches brittle and bare.

Pah-pat-ukale stood nearest to us, a poison arrow already nocked into his bow. He looked over his shoulder as we charged into the clearing, and I saw Dr. Livingston slip behind one of the huge banyan roots on the other side of the clearing. His body was draped with canteens and an oilskin bag that sloshed with water. Before I had time to really wonder why he was bothering to carry such heavy baggage, I saw that he also had my rifle strapped across his back.

"Professor!" Bartley called as he skidded to a stop next to me. "Professor Livingston!"

But there was no answer.

Pah-pat-ukale began to walk on silent cat's feet around the circle of banyan trees, never dropping his bow.

"Professor!" Bartley called again.

There was a shuffle of leaves from the forest where Dr. Livingston had just disappeared.

"He's making a run for it!" I said.

"Look at this place," Lillie said, looking in wonder at the cathedral-like opening in the trees. "Charlie—"

"No time, Lil! Tiger! C'mon! We've got to catch Livingston!"

I headed around the clearing on the other side, ducking and sprinting from trunk to trunk in the banyan maze. I was nervous because nobody knew the accuracy of that rifle better than me. Even Papa said it was one of the finest rifles ever made. I'd found it with Tiger when we were just little boys, hidden in a big oak tree on an old battlefield from the Seminole Wars. It had belonged to Major William Lauderdale and was my prized possession.

But I was also angry. Dr. Livingston had left us for dead in the great swamp, lied to us about his treasure hunt, and now he was trying to slip away again, or maybe even shoot us.

"Dr. Livingston!" I called.

A single shot rang out, and a bullet whizzed through the clearing.

All of us—including Pah-pat-ukale—ducked for cover in the big banyans.

"He's shooting at us!" Bartley said in a shocked voice, hiding behind a huge flared root.

None of us had been hit. When I looked across the clearing, I couldn't see Pah-pat-ukale. I figured he hadn't been hit either.

"Listen up!" Dr. Livingston's voice rang through the clearing. "Bartley! Charlie! I don't want anyone to get hurt here! There's no need for it! But I aim to leave here alone!"

"You lied to us!" Bartley yelled back.

"I want my gun back!" I added.

"You're not getting your gun back!" he said. "As for you, Bartley, I told you back in Connecticut that I didn't want you coming along on this trip! You've no one but yourself to blame for insisting to come!"

"But I thought—"

"Could you stop arguing with the man!" I said. "This ain't a debate." That was one of Papa's favorite sayings.

"Look!" Tiger said quietly, pointing across the clearing.

Banyan trees aren't like other trees. When they get older, they send roots dangling down from their branches toward the ground. When a root touches the ground, it burrows in, and over time, that little wispy root grows into a new trunk. In this way, a single tree can grow to cover a wide piece of ground, with fluted trunks hanging down all over like a maze of columns. These were the biggest banyan trees I'd ever seen, so they had created a maze of columns and trunks supporting the dense canopy.

"I don't see anything," I said.

"There!" Tiger said.

Then I saw him. Pah-pat-ukale was working his way toward Dr. Livingston, creeping between the trunks.

"Dr. Livingston! I mean it!" I shouted. "Unless you put down that rifle, you'll get hurt!"

He barked a short laugh, and another shot rang out through the trees. This time I heard the solid smack of a bullet plowing into the trees and ducked. Lillie looked at me with round eyes, while Bartley huddled on the ground. Across the clearing, Pah-pat-ukale slowed to a crawl, but didn't stop moving.

"You can keep your gold!" I yelled in desperation, hoping no one would get hurt. "You find it, you keep it! No one has to get hurt!"

"Gold?" Dr. Livingston barked. "You still don't understand, do you? This was never about gold."

I was thoroughly befuddled by this statement, but there was no time to discuss it. Soon, Pah-pat-ukale would be within range, and when that happened, I figured the standoff would be over.

A third shot rang out, but he wasn't aiming at us. I saw Pah-pat-ukale drop to the ground, like his legs had been knocked out from under him. I couldn't be sure if he was hit—I didn't see a wound, and he never cried out—but I didn't see him get back up either.

"We've got to split up," I whispered to Tiger. "Lillie, you stay here. And I mean it! Tiger, Dr. Livingston must have the canoe around here somewhere. We need to get it before he can."

"Did he really just shoot that Indian?" Bartley asked in a hollow voice.

"Bartley, can you stay with Lillie?" I asked.

He nodded, still looking shocked.

"Let's go, Charlie," Tiger said, and we crept off toward the shore. I still hadn't heard anything from Pah-pat-ukale, and Dr. Livingston had gone silent. I tried to move as quickly as possible without making too much noise, while Tiger slipped between the banyan roots. I figured Dr. Livingston was headed for the canoe too, and I wanted to get there before him. Once he got onto the open water, it would be impossible to follow him without exposing ourselves. Now I knew he was ready to shoot.

As I neared the edge of the island, I saw that we were on the top of a large crescent-shaped bank that was as tall as me. The big banyans grew right to the edge, their roots crawling like worms down to the sandy beach. Beyond the beach, there were dozens of small islands. It would be an easy thing to get lost in this wilderness.

I hesitated at the top of the bank, balanced on a banyan root. I couldn't see Dr. Livingston around the curve of the island, and I wasn't sure if I should slide down and run along the sandy beach, or if it would be safer to stay hidden among the banyan roots and columns.

I was still trying to make up my mind when I heard Tiger shouting from the beach, "Charlie! Help!"

I jumped down and ran around to the tip of the island, where I saw Tiger standing on the sand, frozen in fear. A huge crocodile, by far the biggest I'd ever seen, was near him on the sand, its head raised and its mouth open. The croc's tail was still in the large hole in the bank where it had been hiding. Tiger must have surprised it.

"Don't move!" I shouted, and the crocodile rose up on its legs like it was getting ready to lunge at Tiger.

While I was trying to figure out what to do, I saw Dr. Livingston. He was in our canoe already, the rifle leaning up against the side while he paddled away.

He glanced over his shoulder and paddled harder.

"Charlie!" Tiger said in fear as the croc hissed at him.

There was a noise on the bank above Tiger, and Lillie appeared.

"Lillie!" I shouted. "No! Get back!"

But she ignored me. Instead, she started pelting the huge croc with stones she had collected. The croc hissed and whipped around, lunging up toward the bank, but it only made it halfway up as she retreated back.

Tiger ran toward me as the croc focused on my little sister.

"Lillie!" I yelled.

I jumped for the bank to crawl up it when I saw Pah-pat-ukale materialize next to her. He glanced down at the hissing, thrashing reptile, then looked out on the water, where Dr. Livingston was making his escape. I couldn't be sure, but I thought Pah-pat-ukale might be bleeding from his side.

I was halfway up the bank, desperate to reach my sister, when another rifle shot rang out, and I slid back down to take cover. Dr. Livingston had stopped paddling and was shooting back at us.

I looked up to make sure Lillie was safe and saw Pah-pat-ukale almost gently lay a hand on her shoulder and pull her back into the darkness of the trees.

The crocodile lunged again, this time making it three quarters of the way up the bank, but still not close enough to grab them. I didn't think it could make it up the embankment, and relief flooded through me.

Pah-pat-ukale raised his bow and put an ar-

row to the string. Instead of aiming at the giant reptile, he raised his bow and took careful aim at Dr. Livingston, who was dropping my rifle back in the bottom of the canoe and picking up his paddle again.

At this distance, there was no way Pah-pat-ukale could hit the professor.

TWANG!

The little arrow sailed through the air like a dart.

TWANG!

Before the first one even landed, Pah-pat-ukale had launched another.

The first one missed, thunking into the side of the canoe. Even from this distance, I saw Dr. Livingston looking at it like he couldn't make sense out of it.

But the next one hit him in the leg. He yelled and grabbed at the slender arrow, pulling it from his leg and tossing it away. They were small, smooth arrows without barbs, not meant to do real damage. After he had thrown the arrow away, Dr. Livingston grabbed the paddle and started to row again.

I hurried up the bank again, with Tiger right behind me. I wanted to find my sister and get away from the crocodile, which had retreated to the water's edge and looked up at the Indian with its mouth still wide open.

As I pulled myself up to the top of the bank, I looked back to see Dr. Livingston wobbling back and forth in the canoe, the paddle trailing uselessly in the water. Then he toppled over in the little boat and disappeared from sight, leaving the canoe drifting aimlessly.

Chapter Seventeen

Under the Cinnamon Tree

In the minute of silence that followed, the crocodile retreated into its nest, vanishing under the bank again to guard its young.

Pah-pat-ukale watched the canoe for a second, then slowly sank to his knees and fell back against a tree. Lillie ran to him and leaned down next to him, grabbing his hand.

"Are you all right, Pah-pat? Are you hurt?"

I stood looking from Pah-pat-ukale to the canoe drifting in the water offshore.

"We have to get that canoe," I said. "Tiger, can you and Bartley go? I don't want to leave Lillie here."

"I go," Tiger said.

"I'll stay," Bartley said, also looking at Pah-pat-ukale. "If he's really hurt, you'll need a translator. Besides, I've no desire to see Dr. Livingston just yet."

"Okay," I answered. "Tiger, be careful. Make sure he's really asleep."

Tiger smiled. "I careful," he said. "No worry."

He walked off down the trail, avoiding the bank where the crocodile had holed up in its nest.

"Charlie, help me," Lillie said, trying to lift up Pah-pat-ukale as he gestured. He wants to go… there." She pointed at the clearing. "Please help me."

I went over and looped an arm under Pah-pat-ukale's arm and helped him up. He grunted a little, but that was it. He had one hand gripped against his side, and I thought I saw a few drops of blood. He leaned on us as he led us back through the banyans into the clearing. Bartley followed.

Once in the clearing, Pah-pat-ukale mo-tioned that he wanted to head for the small, almost dead tree that grew by the basin. We took him to the tree, and he slid down against its trunk like he was sitting in the world's most comfortable and familiar chair. Without knowing exactly how, I was suddenly sure that he had spent many hours sitting under this sad little tree.

Lillie sat down next to him, looking worried while he stared into the bubbling stream.

"Are you hurt?" she asked through Bartley, who stood next to me.

Pah-pat-ukale looked at her, then patted her head and finally spoke. "Not so bad," he said. "I'm just thirsty."

He leaned forward and picked up a polished gourd cup that had been nestled into the thick ferns. He dipped it into the basin of clear water, then raised it to his lips and took a deep drink. Afterward, he leaned back and closed his eyes. A small smile played around his lips, and the look of pain vanished. The color seemed to flood back into his face.

I sat down next to Pah-pat-ukale in the shadow of the little tree. A wonderful smell surrounded me, faint but familiar. I breathed deeply, then it hit me. Cinnamon! It smelled like Christmas morning and the buttered cinnamon rolls that Mama always made. A sudden wave of homesickness washed over me, and I found myself smiling at Lillie, happy that she was safe and unharmed.

"What?" she said. "Why are you looking at me like that?"

Pah-pat-ukale opened his eyes and smiled at me, like a teacher who is happy when a student learns something new.

"What is this place?" I asked, as Bartley translated.

The old Indian looked up into the little tree, a sad smile creasing his face.

"This is the spiritual home of the Calusa," he said. "And now it is like me, fading and old. When I was young, this tree was full of leaves. We have seen many seasons together, this tree and I." He looked down and took another long drink of water. I couldn't be sure, but his color looked better, and he sat up straighter, like he wasn't in so much pain anymore, like he was already starting to heal. He went on. "This place is where the endless cycle of life begins. This is the place where the sky and the earth first came together and created the spring that gives eternal life."

Bartley hardly finished translating before he whispered, "It can't be!"

"What can't be?" I asked.

But Bartley didn't answer. Instead, he walked toward the spring and knelt next to it, hovering his hand over it like he was warming his hands over embers. Now Pah-pat-ukale turned his knowing smile on Bartley.

Bartley turned back and said something to Pah-pat-ukale in Spanish, then translated for us: "I asked him how old he really is."

"As old as the trees," Pah-pat-ukale said. "Old enough to have outlived everyone I loved."

"Bartley," I said. "What's going on?"

"Charlie," he said. "Don't you get it? Professor Livingston was telling the truth. It was never about gold. It was about this place."

"No, I don't get it," I said. "What about this place? I mean, it's a nice place, and there are plenty of springs and trees—"

Before Bartley could respond, Pah-pat-ukale

spoke again. "The man," he said, "the one in the canoe. How did he find me?"

"He had a map," I answered, distracted. "In a book."

"Does he still have it? I want to see it."

"I don't know," I said. "I'd guess so. Bartley, what's going on?"

Then all of a sudden, the bits and pieces of the puzzle fell into place and the hairs on my arms and neck raised. I thought about Dr. Livingston with his map book, how he was draped with canteens and an oilskin bag full of water as he ran away. I thought about him yelling that it was never about gold. About this place, with its huge trees and giant crocodiles. And about Ponce de León, the Spanish explorer.

I remembered a book Mama had read to me as a child about the legends of the old explorers. There was a drawing in the book showing Ponce de León on his quest for the mythical Fountain of Youth in Florida. But that was just a children's story, just a thing they wrote stories about like unicorns or machines that flew through the air.

Then I looked down at the little spring bubbling up in the rock, and shock flooded through me as the full understanding settled on me like a blanket.

Pah-pat-ukale watched us as we each had the

same realization in our own way. Lillie's hand flew up to her mouth, and Bartley stood and walked around the spring in a circle, staring up into the trees with their thick mat of plants covering their branches.

No one spoke until Pah-pat-ukale said, "This spring has been the strength of my people since the dawn of time. This is where we learned to take only what we need from the land and water, so there will always be plenty. But now the world has changed. The time of the Calusa has passed, and when I go to the spirit world, it will be over. The white man and the white man's ways will take over the world."

"What does that mean?" Lillie asked. "Why do you make that sound so bad?"

"Not bad," he said. "But it is different. The white man's way is change. The white man is known for the power of his will, and his will is mighty indeed. He will look at this place and see only what he can change. He will cut down the trees he needs to make his buildings, which will be larger than the biggest home the cacique ever made. He will look at the water and only think of what he can take from it. His whole world will be known not by the way things are, but by the way he wants them to be. He will become more numerous than the stars in the sky."

I pictured our home and our cleared fields and a stab of guilt went through me, but I didn't really understand what I had to feel guilty about. "But," I said, waiting for Bartley to translate, "it sounds like you don't want any progress."

Pah-pat-ukale shook his head. "Progress? What is this progress?"

"What is progress?" Bartley cut in, translating for us while he talked. "Progress means we'll soon be able to board a train in New York and make it to California in just a few days. It means better medicines and less hunger, less disease and better conditions for all men. It means increasing our understanding of the natural world through the application of science."

Pah-pat-ukale smiled and looked down. "This progress sounds wonderful, as hard to stop as the sunset or sunrise. But I do not need it to understand the world."

Just then, Tiger came back up the trail. He had my rifle propped over his shoulder, and he was whistling as he walked. He held Dr. Livingston's jacket in one hand and stopped whistling every few steps to take a bite of a thick slab of beef jerky.

"Charlie," Tiger said. "Dr. Livingston still sleeping. Look. From the canoe." He held out more jerky. "Want some?"

I took a piece and chewed it absentmindedly while I thought about what Pah-pat-ukale had said. What was so wrong with progress? But then I also remembered the islands of dead birds killed by the white plume hunters, and then I thought of the lakeshore around Hypoluxo Island, where pineapple farms were replacing forest that had once teemed with deer and rabbits and where more and more homesteads spread over the best land. I wanted to ask, wasn't it possible to have both? Why not?

Then I remembered something else Pah-pat-ukale had said and asked Tiger for Dr. Livingston's jacket. Sure enough, the map book was still in his pocket. I pulled it out and handed it to the Calusa.

Pah-pat-ukale flipped it open and leafed through the pages, holding the book on its side and upside down. He couldn't read.

"I think it's Ponce de León's," I said.

"That is a name I recognize," Pah-pat-ukale said, frowning as he flipped to the section with the maps. Then, before anyone said a word, he suddenly ripped the maps from the book and crumpled them up. Then he threw the ball of paper into the spring and we all watched as the soggy, ancient paper dissolved into threads and flowed away on the fast current.

"There is my progress," he said, almost to himself. When he looked up again, his face was set, his expression hard.

"Now," he said, "you must go and never come back. And if you do come back, don't expect to find anything. All of this will be gone."

"But—" Lillie said.

"No," he said, softening a little and laying a

hand on her head. "Even you. It is time for you all to go."

Lillie looked like she wanted to argue, but instead she stood up, along with me, Tiger, and Bartley.

"Good-bye," she said, and Bartley didn't bother to translate as Pah-pat-ukale raised his hand in farewell, then motioned for us to leave.

We walked down the same path we had come in, and at the last minute, before we turned out of sight, I looked back over my shoulder in time to see Pah-pat-ukale rise silently to his feet like he'd never been hurt at all. He poured out his little gourd cup on the ground, then dabbed a bit of the clear spring water on his forehead, and his lips moved with silent words.

Finally, he turned and walked away into the banyans. I blinked as his image wavered, seeming to disappear and reappear, and then with a final flicker, Pah-pat-ukale disappeared, never to be seen again.

Epilogue

The trip out of the swamp was much faster, as we headed directly back to the river and back to the *Creole.*

I told Dr. Livingston we wouldn't bind his hands any longer, but he had to promise to stay with us. He agreed without much emotion, like he had fallen under a dark cloud, and in truth, none of us talked about much in the days we traveled back to the boat.

One evening, while we were making camp, Dr. Livingston looked at me and said, "You know, Charlie, now we'll never know."

"Never know what?" I asked.

"If that spring really was the Fountain of Youth. It may have been."

I thought about that for a second, stirring the fire with a stick. Then I said, "I guess that's alright by me. Maybe we weren't supposed to know."

But the trip wasn't a complete failure. On the way off Banyan Island, Bartley had stopped to quickly collect a few magnificent orchids from the trees there and wrap them in damp moss.

His Wardian case was long gone, but he thought he could keep the orchids alive long enough to get back to the boat, where he built a new case from spare lumber. It was nice to see him excited again.

And we did end up getting paid for the trip. Once we arrived home, Papa sat down with Dr. Livingston and figured up all the expenses. Then Dr. Livingston paid Tiger in cash and wrote a bank draft to a "Mr. Charlie Pierce." The next morning, Dr. Livingston and Bartley were back on the ferry to the north end of the lake, where a carriage was waiting to take them to catch the rail home.

I used the money to buy the violin I had my eye on, and I started learning on it right away. I kept that violin for the rest of my life.

A few months later, we were surprised to see a messenger coming over on a ferry, waving at us. He had a package for us marked "Yale University."

None of us knew what to expect as we gathered around the kitchen table while Papa cut the string and opened the paper. Inside, there was a magazine and single sheet of paper. Papa held the paper up and read out loud:

Charlie and Lillie,
  I hope this letter finds you well. This magazine is the official scientific journal of the emerging discipline of Botany. I will never forget all that happened during our travels, and it has given me great cause to think. Please turn to page 104.
  Your Friend,
Jonathan Bartley

Papa flipped the magazine open, and Mama gasped and held her hand to her chest. "My word! It's lovely! And Lillie! Look!"

Papa set the journal down on the table so we could all see the drawing of a beautiful purple flower with black bumps on its smooth petals. Underneath it, the caption read, "A new species of orchid, *P. Lilliensis*, discovered by J. Bartley, Assistant Professor, Yale University."

Mama and Papa were so proud of Lillie and her flower that we never had the heart to tell them what really happened in the great swamp.

But I still thought about it all the time, especially when I was out in the woods or sailing along the lakeshore. Papa told me there was talk of building a great rail line running all the way down to the Keys. He said such a railway would be progress for the whole region, that it would bring more people down and let Uncle Will ship out his pineapples and other goods to the north.

I nodded along, but in my heart, I thought about what Pah-pat-ukale had said and wondered what would happen to the wild forests, the clear waters, and the long, open beaches of the lake country once a rail had stitched its way down here.

I guess I would just have to wait and find out.

Postscript

The Calusa Indians

Pah-pat-ukale is a fictional character, but the Calusa Indians were a very real people. The Calusa lived in South Florida long before European explorers discovered the New World. Their main villages were on the west coast of Florida, near present-day Fort Myers and Charlotte Harbor. From there, they controlled territory stretching north from present-day Tampa across the modern Everglades and as far away as the Florida Keys and Lake Okeechobee.

The Calusa were master fishermen and lived off the sea. They used nets, spears, fishhooks made from bone, and other tools to catch all kinds of fish. They also harvested shellfish and are credited with digging many miles of canals by hand to connect parts of their vast territory.

Today, the Calusa are most famous for their shell mounds, which are known as middens. Archaeologists have learned that the Calusa built their houses on top of these mounds. One such building that belonged to the Calusa great chief, or cacique, was big enough to hold an estimated two thousand people at once! Archaeologists believe the Calusa used palm thatch to make roofs, just like the Seminole Indians, although no Calusa buildings exist today to verify this belief.

The Calusa were great artists. Scientists have discovered many pieces of Calusa art, including carvings made from bone and wood and many things used in daily life like cups and fishing tools.

They were also very brave warriors. The Calusa fiercely resisted the European soldiers and explorers who came to their lands, including the famous Spaniard Ponce de León. However, they could not resist the diseases brought by Europeans or defeat the modern weapons of the Europeans. It is believed the last of the Calusa people faded from the historical record in the late 1700s as other Native American tribes, such as the Seminoles, migrated into the areas they once controlled.

Today, there are no Calusa left and their language has disappeared, but they remain perhaps the civilization that endured in Florida the longest.

Juan Ponce de León

Juan Ponce de León first traveled to the land that he would name Florida in the spring of 1513. There is no clear record that de León was actually in search of or found the Fountain of Youth. That story surfaced in 1535, more than twenty years later, when a historian named Gonzalo Fernandez de Oviedo y Valdes wrote in his book, *La Natural hystoria de las Indias*, that de León was searching for the legendary Fountain of Youth. After that first mention, many historians repeated the story, until an influential historian named Antonio de Herrera y Tordesillas included the story in his history of the Spanish in the New World. Ever since, many people have believed de León was in Florida looking for the Fountain of Youth, even though we don't really know for sure.

About Charlie Pierce

Charles William Pierce was born in Waukegan, Illinois in 1864 and moved with his parents to Jupiter, Florida in 1872 at the age of eight years when his father was given the job as assistant keeper of the Jupiter Lighthouse. At the time, South Florida was a wild jungle frontier inhabited almost entirely by Seminole Indians.

The Pierce family homesteaded Hypoluxo Island in 1873 and built a house made of salvaged shipwreck timbers with a palmetto frond thatched roof.

Left to right: Margretta M. Pierce; Hannibal D. Pierce; Andrew W. Garnett; James "Ed" Hamilton; Lillie E. Pierce; and Charles W. Pierce at the Pierce family home on Hypoluxo Island, ca. 1886. *Photo courtesy of Historical Society of Palm Beach County*

In 1876, Charlie's sister, Lillie, was born. She was the first white child ever born between Jupiter and Miami, an area that contains approximately seven million people today. In 1878, the Pierces were one of the families that salvaged some twenty thousand coconuts from the wreck of the Spanish ship *Providencia* and planted them all over the barrier islands. The coconuts would later give Palm Beach, West Palm Beach, and Palm Beach County their names.

The mailman in this mural titled *The Barefoot Mailman*, by Stevan Dohanos, is said to resemble Charlie Pierce. *Photo courtesy of Historical Society of Palm Beach County*

During his long, illustrious career, Charlie Pierce served in many capacities, including as a boat captain, bank president, farmer, school district trustee, postmaster, and most notably as one of the legendary Barefoot Mailmen. His childhood adven-

170

tures were accurately recorded, and his writings remain today one of the best firsthand accounts of early exploration in southeast Florida. Pierce was farsighted enough to maintain a daily journal from early childhood until late in his life. These journal entries provide the foundation for his book, *Pioneer Life in Southeast Florida*, which is the most comprehensive account of the pioneer settlement of South Florida and the primary reference for most subsequent books on the region's history.

Charles Pierce at his desk, ca. 1930. *Photo courtesy of Historical Society of Palm Beach County*

Pierce died in 1939, at age seventy-five, while still serving as the postmaster of Boynton Beach.   Pierce Hammock Elementary School in Palm Beach County is named in his honor. In 2009, the State of Florida posthumously named Charles Pierce a "Great Floridian," one of fewer than sixty people in Florida's history granted that title.

About the Author

Harvey E. Oyer III is a fifth-generation Floridian and is descended from one of the earliest pioneer families in South Florida. He is the great-great-grandson of Captain Hannibal Dillingham Pierce and his wife, Margretta Moore Pierce, who in 1872 became one of the first non-Native American families to settle in southeast Florida. Oyer is the great-grandnephew of Charlie Pierce, the subject of this book. Oyer is an attorney in West Palm Beach, Florida, a Cambridge University-educated archaeologist, and an avid historian. He served for many years as the chairman of the Historical Society of Palm Beach County, currently serves on the board of the Florida Historical Society, has written or contributed to numerous books and articles about Florida history, and was named Florida's Distinguished Author in 2013. Many of the stories contained in this book have been passed down through five generations of his family.

Harvey E. Oyer III

For more information about the author, Harvey E. Oyer III, or Charlie Pierce and his adventures, go to **www.TheAdventuresofCharliePierce.com**

Become a friend of Charlie Pierce on **Facebook**

Facebook.com/CharliePierceBooks

Visit The Adventures of Charlie Pierce website at
www.TheAdventuresofCharliePierce.com

- The Adventures Continue Online
- Learn More About the Real-life Charlie, Tiger, and Lillie
- Play Games
- Watch Videos
- Find All of the Charlie Pierce Books Online
- Additional Teaching Materials
- And Much, Much More...

The Adventures of Charlie Pierce Collection

The Adventures of Charlie Pierce: The American Jungle
Seminoles, Spanish Treasure & The American Jungle

In 1872, eight-year-old Charlie Pierce arrived with his Mama and Papa in the frontier jungles of South Florida. Charlie's adventures began right away. In this account, based on actual diaries, he explores old battlefields, learns to hunt and boat like a Seminole, faces down hurricanes, and makes an incredible discovery in the sand.

The Adventures of Charlie Pierce: The Last Egret
America's Greatest Environmental Adventure Story for Children

In the late nineteenth century, hunters killed millions of birds in the Florida Everglades to supply the booming trade in bird feathers for ladies' fashion. As teenagers, Charlie Pierce and his friends traveled deep into the unexplored Florida Everglades to hunt plume birds for their feathers. They never imagined the challenges they would encounter, what they would learn about themselves, and how they would contribute to American history.

The Adventures of Charlie Pierce: The Last Calusa
Discover What Lies Hidden in America's Secret River

When famous scientist Dr. George Livingston shows up in the steamy jungles of Florida, he makes teenage Charlie Pierce a very generous offer. He'll pay Charlie $5 a day to guide him and his young assistant deep into the Everglades in search of the rare ghost orchid. But it doesn't take long before the expedition discovers that the swamp is hiding much more than a rare flower as the oldest legends suddenly spring to life.

The Adventures of Charlie Pierce: The Barefoot Mailman
The Mail Must Go!

Charlie Pierce isn't looking for an adventure when he agrees to help out his friend and neighbor Ed Hamilton. Hamilton's job is to walk the U.S. Mail from Palm Beach to Miami and back every week, following a dangerous route that cuts through the jungle and across the water. When Hamilton goes missing, it's up to Charlie and his sister, Lillie, to retrace Hamilton's steps and find out what happened to the missing Barefoot Mailman.

Awards for The Adventures of Charlie Pierce

Florida Publishers Association

Gold Medal - Children's Fiction (*The American Jungle*, 2010)
Gold Medal - Florida Children's Book (*The American Jungle*, 2010)
Gold Medal - Children's Fiction (*The Last Egret*, 2011)
Silver Medal - Florida Children's Book (*The Last Egret*, 2011)
Gold Medal - Florida Children's Book (*The Last Calusa*, 2013)
Silver Medal - Children's Fiction (*The Last Calusa*, 2013)
Gold Medal - Fiction/Non-Fiction: Juvenile (*The Barefoot Mailman*, 2015)

James J. Horgan Award (Florida Historical Society)

(*The Last Egret*, 2011)
(*The Last Calusa*, 2013)
(*Charlie and the Tycoon*, 2017)

Florida Book Award

Bronze Medal - Children's Literature (*The Last Egret*, 2010)

Mom's Choice Awards

Silver Medal (*The Last Egret*, 2010)